Sport Crazy

Sport Crazy

Des Lynam

with Mike Lepine & Mark Leigh

C

Century · London

First published by Century in 1998

1 3 5 7 9 10 8 6 4 2

First published in the United Kingdom in 1998 by Century
Random House, 20 Vauxhall Bridge Road,
London SW1V 2SA

Random House Australia (Pty) Ltd
20 Alfred Street, Milsons Point, Sydney,
New South Wales 2061, Australia

Random House New Zealand Limited
18 Poland Road, Glenfield, Auckland 10, New Zealand

Random House South Africa (Pty) Limited
Endulini, 5a Jubilee Road, Parktown 2193, South Africa

Random House UK Limited Reg. No. 954009

A CIP catalogue record for this book is
available from the British Library

Papers used by Random House UK are natural, recyclable
products made from wood grown in sustainable forests. The
manufacturing processes conform to the environmental
regulations of the country of origin.

ISBN 0 7126 8050 0

Illustrations © Terry Carter

Design and make-up by Roger Walker
Set in Adobe Minion, Quay Sans and Remedy

Printed and bound in Great Britain by Redwood Books

Contents

Acknowledgements

The authors would like to thank the following people for their invaluable help and assistance:

Susie Alexander, Rob Bagchi, Angela Bastable, Jeremy Beadle, Terry Carter, Anna Cherrett, Perry Cohn, Gary Fairhead, Danny Gregorious, Graham Hart, Mary Hatton, Philippa Hatton-Lepine, Mike Innes, Debbie Leigh, David Landau, Neville and Gill Landau, Harold and Eileen Lepine, Ian Marshall, Judy Martin, Kate Parkin, Liz Rowlinson, Terry Unwin and John Wright.

Cartoons by Terry Carter.

introduction

Results don't tell you much. Who won. Who lost. Who beat the record. If you're only interested in the results, you're missing out. You may know that the 18-year-old Cassius Clay beat three times European Champion Zbigniew Pietrzykowski by a unanimous 5–0 decision to take gold at the 1960 Olympic Games in Rome...

...but did you know that Clay only became a boxer because he had his bicycle stolen?

You might be the sort who can recite the exact score from every Test England has ever played...

...but did you know that overarm bowling was invented by a woman? Or that the man who created Sherlock Holmes once bowled out the great WG Grace?

Outrageous personalities. Extraordinary events. Wild and improbable coincidences. Moments of unintentional hilarity or high drama or complete madness. People at their very best – or worst. Now that's sport. It's trivia – but it's glorious trivia.

Enjoy the book.

Des Lynam, 1998

CHAPTER 1

We Was Robbed!

**'I don't know why everything keeps going wrong.
Somebody at Team Lotus must have run over a nun'**
– Jochen Rindt

Two New York lawyers were keen runners and decided to settle a bet about who was the fastest over 100 metres by running down an office corridor. One of them, though, had forgotten to wear his contact lenses and he overshot the designated finish, crashing through a plate glass window and falling 39 floors to his death.

★　★　★

It was the 1978 World Cup. Scotland had drawn 1–1 with Iran and it looked like the Scots were on their way home on the next plane. Public opinion was already turning against the manager. 'Ally MacLeod believes that tactics are a new form of peppermint' was a cruel but popular joke in Scotland at the time.

In the stadium, Ally MacLeod sat with his head in his hands, all alone, as Scotland's dream crumbled before him. As he sat there, a small cute dog scampered up to him. 'Ah, my only wee friend in the entire world,' Ally said. The dog bit him.

✦ ✦ ✦

Pedro Gatica was a true fan of his national team, Argentina. Too poor to fly or even to catch the train to see his beloved country compete in the 1986 World Cup, he cycled all the way to Mexico. When he arrived in Mexico City, he went straight to the ticket office – only to find that the tickets were too expensive for him. Crushed, he decided there and then he had no choice but to cycle home again. Unfortunately, someone had stolen his bicycle while he was at the ticket office…

✦ ✦ ✦

A couple of weeks after being sent off during a 1995 local league match in southern Italy, a letter was sent to footballer Luigi Coluccio, informing him that he was suspended because of his disciplinary record. That was the least of his worries however. Nine days earlier he had been killed in a Mafia-related shooting.

✦ ✦ ✦

It was the last few minutes of the December 1955 football match between Arsenal and Blackpool. Arsenal were leading 4–0 and absolutely confident of victory. Dennis Evans, Arsenal's full back, was starting to relax. He heard the whistle blow and volleyed the ball into the back of his own net in relief. All the other players – and the referee – stared at him in disbelief. The whistle had come from the crowd, not the referee – and the goal stood.

✦ ✦ ✦

The family of 60-year-old linesman Richard Wertheim tried to sue the US Tennis Association for $2 million after he was hit in the groin by a ball hit by Stefan Edberg. The shot at the 1983 US Open Junior Final was so powerful that, apart from bringing tears to his eyes, it knocked him to the ground where he fractured his skull on the hard surface. The case was eventually thrown out by a New York court in 1989.

It sounds crazy but a fly decided the outcome of the world billiards championship in September 1865. The final was between Louis Fox and John Deery, each determined to win the $40,000 prize money at stake. Crowds jammed the ballroom of the Washington Hotel to see the match. Pundits forecast an even game but to his opponent's horror, Fox stormed off to a huge lead and soon had victory within his sight.

Potting ball after ball, there seemed no stopping him, but then a fly, which had been buzzing around the ballroom all afternoon, descended on the cue ball. Fox shooed it away with his hand but it came back. He did it again but still the fly came back. The third time he waved his cue to shoo it away – and accidentally hit the cue ball, committing a foul shot. By moving the cue ball, Fox forfeited his chance to continue, giving Deery a chance to get back into the game. Deery didn't look back and sunk every shot, eventually winning the contest. Louis Fox never recovered from this defeat at the hands (or legs) of a fly. He left the hotel disconsolate and was found by police the next day, drowned.

 Hibs have 66 players on their books – that's a team for every day of the week except Saturday.
– *An anonymous supporter, criticising Hibernian's dismal performance in the 1990–91 season*

One of the most unforgettable images from the Olympic Games is the sight of the Italian marathon runner Dorando Pietri, having given his all, being helped by stewards across the finishing line at the 1908 London Games. He'd entered the White City Stadium after his run, seeming to have no idea where he was. Just 385 yards from the finish line, he headed in completely the wrong direction, then collapsed on the track, got up, staggered on a few yards, and collapsed again.

One alarmed official later explained why they went to his aid. 'It was impossible to leave him there,' he said, 'for it looked as if he might die in the very presence of the Queen!' In the end, officials and well wishers including head organiser Jack Andrew and Sir Arthur Conan Doyle, creator of Sherlock Holmes, supported the semi-conscious Italian over the finish line. Pietri was declared the winner, and the Italian flag raised in his honour as he lay on a stretcher, but the American competitors complained and their objection was upheld.

Pietri was awarded a special gold cup by Queen Alexandra for his heroic efforts and was treated almost universally as a hero. Almost. Famous composer Irving Berlin, obviously having a bit of an off day, wrote a sarcastic, racist and abusive song about the heroic runner entitled 'Dorando He's a Gooda for Not!' and accusing him of being a 'bigga de flop'.

The official winner of the race was John Hayes, an American who used to train on a special track constructed on the roof of Bloomingdale's department store where he worked as a clerk. Later, Hayes ran against Pietri in two special marathons held in New York to determine the real champion of champions. On both occasions the Italian won. Hayes went on to become a wealthy man, while Pietri had his money stolen by his brother and had to work as a taxi driver for the rest of his life…

★ ★ ★

Some days it just doesn't pay to get out of bed. In 1982, Bristol City defender Rob Newman had precisely one of those days. He managed to score no fewer than two own goals against his team and then returned utterly dejected to the dressing room, only to find someone had stolen his wallet…

★ ★ ★

In 1963, Jim Armstrong teed off at the second hole at the Desert Forest Golf Club in Carefree, Arizona. His shot hit a tee marker and ricocheted straight back into his face, knocking him senseless for a few moments. Recovering, he teed off again. The ball hit the same post, ricocheted back again and smashed into his knee. He abandoned the game.

A very similar thing happened in 1936 at the Victoria Golf Club in Cheltenham, Australia. Carl Klinger's drive hit a

telegraph pole, rebounded and landed right next to him. He took another shot and it hit the same pole – this time, though, it rebounded and fractured his nose.

★　★　★

Smoke billowed out from the trousers of Australian batsman Stan Dawson during a match at Kalgoorlie in the late 1970s. It wasn't because of his speed – just the fact that the ball had hit a packet of matches in his hip pocket which then burst into flames. As if that wasn't bad enough, he was run out as he desperately tried to beat out the flames rapidly licking across his groin.

★　★　★

Former British Lion John Rutherford was courageous on the rugby field but a bag of nerves in TV interviews. To help him, a veteran broadcaster told him just to 'concentrate on your opening sentence, and the rest will all fall into place'. Shortly afterwards he was invited to appear on TV to talk about a recent Scottish tour of Australia and New Zealand. John had enough notice to write and rehearse over and over again his opening line, 'I've just returned from New Zealand where rugby is more a religion than a sport'. By the time he was on air he was cool, calm and collected. Then the interviewer introduced him by saying, 'With me tonight is John Rutherford who's just returned from New Zealand, where rugby is more a religion than a sport…'

★　★　★

It was man against machine when Torquay cricketer Martyn Goulding took net practice to get ready for the 1995–96 season. He was facing the automatic bowling machine when one of the

75 mph deliveries caught him on his foot, breaking it. As if that wasn't bad enough, as he lay on the ground in agony the machine then delivered another high speed ball to his chest, breaking two ribs.

* * *

In 1927 a US football team with the grand name of the Providence Steamrollers invited Perry Jackson, an Oklahoma college football star, for a trial. At the time Jackson was very ill so he sent a friend, Arnold Schockley, along instead. Schockley was a fair player, but not as good as Jackson. However, the ruse worked and Schockley became a regular player in the team that won the 1928 National Football League. Once he'd fully recovered from his illness, Jackson had a trial for the team, this time calling himself Arnold Schockley. He didn't make it.

* * *

Sometimes you can be a little too sporting, as American pole vaulter Earl Bell found out at the 1976 US Olympic trials. At the time Bell held the world record in the event at 18 feet $7\frac{1}{4}$ inches. He lent his vaulting pole to fellow athlete Dave Roberts to see if it would help him make the team; it did, and in the process Roberts broke Bell's record by an inch.

* * *

One of the most unusual exhibits on display at the museum at Lord's is a stuffed sparrow perched on top of a cricket ball. The unfortunate bird was struck a mortal injury by a ball bowled by Jehengir Khan in 1936 at a match between the MCC and Cambridge University. The incident led to *The Times* solemnly commenting that 'it is extraordinary that the rate of mortality of sparrows on cricket grounds is not higher'.

★ ★ ★

Scottish Club Greenock Morton were sure that their new mascot, Toby the Sheep, was a good-luck charm. On his first appearance for the club in 1910 they won convincingly. Sadly, though, Toby wasn't as lucky as everyone had thought. He was left unattended in the changing rooms after the match and drowned in the communal bath.

★ ★ ★

In the July 1912 boxing world lightweight title fight between 'Wildcat' Al Wolgast and Joe Rivers, both boxers managed to deliver a crushing knockout blow to each other at exactly the same moment in the thirteenth round. As the two fighters lay in a heap, referee Joe Welch made one of

the most controversial decisions in boxing history. He raised Wolgast's limp left arm, declaring him the champ – because he was lying on top of Rivers!

Stanley Pinto thought he knew the ropes when it came to wrestling but in one fight they caused his downfall – literally. He managed to get himself caught up in them and then tripped over, pinning both his shoulders to the canvas. The referee counted the required three seconds and declared his opponent, who hadn't laid a finger on Stanley, the winner.

Japanese golfer Kano Yashamura was responsible for a hole in one, but didn't live to tell the tale, let alone know about it. It happened in 1992 when a ball struck by someone else's 220-yard drive hit him on the head, killing him instantly, and then bounced straight into the hole.

A Zimbabwean golfer going by the unlikely name of Eugenius Wimple was so excited after hitting a hole in one that he leapt into his electric golf cart and drove round and round in sheer delight. Unfortunately, Eugenius drove over a small rise and crashed into the makeshift bamboo toilet concealed behind it. Four people were using it at the time and one of his victims later told the press, 'One minute I was on the loo, the next I was straddling a golf buggy. Next time I'll go in the bloody bushes!'

A pigeon race held in Taiwan in June 1984 got off to a promising start when over 2,000 birds were released. By the end of the race only ten returned home – the remaining 1,990 were caught in huge nets en route an hour after the race began and ended up at local restaurants.

* * *

In the 1966–67 football season Colchester United half back Bobby Blackwood broke his jaw in a violent collision with QPR striker Les Allen. He was declared fit in time to play in the return match – only to collide with Les Allen again, breaking his jaw once more!

* * *

When a South African boxer named Hamilton-Brown lost his first bout at the 1936 Olympics on a split decision, he was crushed. He'd endured months of punishing training and fasting for nothing. Thoroughly disheartened, he consoled himself with a night of frantic binge eating – not knowing that one of the judges had accidentally got his scores muddled up and that Hamilton-Brown was really the winner. The Olympic authorities reinstated him for the next round – but by then it was too late. Hamilton-Brown had put on more than five pounds thanks to his bingeing and no longer made the limit for his weight class. He had to be disqualified.

* * *

When veteran racing driver Buddy Baker's Dodge blew a tyre and smashed into a concrete barrier during a race at the Smoky Mountain Raceway in Tennessee in 1968, it was only the

beginning of his problems. Concussed and with broken ribs, Baker was helped on to a rolling stretcher, securely strapped in and bundled into the back of a waiting ambulance. As it pulled away however, the rear doors swung open and Baker found himself rolling out of the ambulance on the stretcher – right on to the racetrack. As the stretcher rolled across the track, racing cars roared past him left and right, missing him by inches.

★   ★   ★

As a special Mother's Day Treat, the famous Cleveland baseball star Bob Feller brought his mum all the way from her farm in Iowa to Chicago to watch him pitch in a major league game. She had never seen her son play professionally before and so was thrilled to go. Early in the game, however, her son hurled a fast pitch to a Chicago White Sox batter, who hit it into the stands. Of course, out of the 45,000 spectators at the game, the ball had to strike Feller's mother right on the head, knocking her unconscious. She never attended another game.

* * *

Cricketer David Pritchard was leaving
the pavilion to bat in a charity match
in 1988 when he was knocked out.
It wasn't by a stray ball but the
number '0' that had blown
off the scoreboard and
hit him on the head.

* * *

In 1896, Italy decided not to field a team at the Athens Olympics.
However, national pride got the better of one Italian athlete, who
decided he would go and defend his country's honour anyway.
He had no money, so he decided to walk all the way from his
home in Milan. It was a long and arduous journey over dusty

roads that were little more than tracks, often in blazing heat. More than once along the way, the athlete nearly succumbed to thirst and hunger, but he kept going – he had to race. Against the odds he made it to the Games, and in time to take part. Unfortunately, when he got there, he couldn't prove he was an amateur and was automatically disqualified.

American runner Kim Jones was leading in the Sapporo marathon in Japan in August 1992 when bad luck struck. After nine miles she stopped for refreshment but dropped her water bottle. As she bent over to pick it up she put her back out and had to retire from the race.

British runner John Oliver had worse luck. He'd travelled 5,000 miles from his home town of Bournemouth in Dorset to take part in the Nepal marathon, only to sprain his ankle at the starting line.

It was to be the sporting achievement of a lifetime for cyclist Michael Murphy. He would circle the globe on a bike and set a new world record. At times on his epic journey the obstacles seemed insurmountable. Peasants in Yugoslavia mugged him. Afghan tribesmen tried to stone him to death and he almost perished in a blizzard in the heart of the Himalayas. But somehow, through courage, ingenuity – and maybe a stroke or two of luck – the electrician

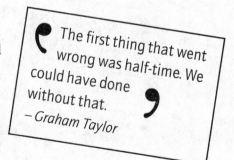

The first thing that went wrong was half-time. We could have done without that.
– Graham Taylor

from Stevenage managed to make it through. After 25,000 miles on his bike, he finally started to relax as his plane touched down at Heathrow. All he had to do now was cycle home and the world record was his. As he stood, waiting to be reunited with the bike that had taken him around the world, he was approached by two rather sheepish Heathrow employees. It transpired that his trusty bike had been accidentally mangled beyond repair by the cargo conveyor belt – and with it went his world record.

★ ★ ★

Legendary footballer William Ralph Dean, better known as Dixie Dean, was playing for Tranmere when a Rochdale defender kicked him in the groin, laying him out flat. To ease the pain, one of Dean's teammates started to rub the affected area, at which point Dean looked down and said, 'Never mind bloody rubbing them – count 'em!'

In 1991 the Real Madrid player Michel received a fine for grabbing the testicles of Carlos Valderrama, who was playing for Valladolid. After they'd passed judgement, the disciplinary committee issued a statement where they described the act as 'publicly manipulating the gift nature only gives to men'.

> I've given up cricket for sex – because the scoring's easier and you don't have to change shoes.
> – Freddie Trueman

CHAPTER 2
Total Humiliation

'Trevor Brooking floats like a butterfly, and stings like one too'
– Brian Clough

It was England versus the West Indies. Michael Holding was bowling to Peter Willey. So what else could Brian Johnston say from the commentary box but, 'The bowler's Holding, the batsman's Willey.' You could commentate all your life and not get a chance to make a gaffe as good as that one.

★ ★ ★

Every professional sports commentator has done it at some time. During the legendary 1974 'rumble in the jungle' heavyweight boxing match in Zaire between Muhammad Ali and George Foreman, it just happened to be Harry Carpenter's turn. Watching from the ringside, Harry told the world, 'That's it. There's no way Ali can win this one now.' Ali promptly knocked Foreman out...

★ ★ ★

When it came to his performance in the marathon, Wallace Williams of the Virgin Islands was slow but sure. In the 1979 Pan American games held in Puerto Rico he arrived back at the stadium nearly 45 minutes after the last runner, only to find he couldn't get in. The officials had forgotten about him, locked up and gone home.

★   ★   ★

The only man ever to knock out world champion boxer Jack Dempsey was oil billionaire John Paul Getty I. The two got into a heated row over a girl and the plucky Getty knocked Dempsey out cold with a left uppercut.

★   ★   ★

Sensing how dejected and down Ken Norton was after his 1976 defeat by Muhammad Ali, Harry Carpenter consoled him by saying, 'If you hadn't been there it wouldn't have been much of a fight…'

★   ★   ★

Champion Russian ice hockey goalkeeper Vladislav Tretiak had to retire from the 1981 USSR National Championships when he fractured his leg getting off a bus. How? He slipped on a patch of ice.

★   ★   ★

Temperamental golfer Tom Bolt was famous for throwing his clubs away in disgust when he played badly and, during the 1960 Open in Denver, he was playing worse than usual. After knocking two successive balls into the lake, he threw his driver in after them. Almost immediately, a small boy ran out of the crowd, jumped into the lake, dived under the water and reappeared holding Bolt's club. The crowd were cheering wildly and

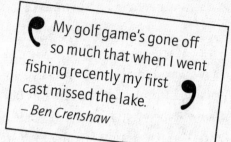

My golf game's gone off so much that when I went fishing recently my first cast missed the lake.
– Ben Crenshaw

even Tom Bolt couldn't resist a smile. He calmed down and went over to the little boy to thank him – at which point the boy gave him the finger and ran off happily brandishing the golf club.

★ ★ ★

It wasn't common knowledge that, in real life, veteran New Jersey sports writer Bob Harding had a stutter. Equally, it wasn't common knowledge that Chicago Bulls player Bob Love had a stutter as well. Both were understandably very sensitive about the problem, but refused to let it dominate their lives.

Visiting New Jersey, Bob Love agreed to an interview by Bob Harding. The two men sat down together and Harding stuttered out the first question. Love couldn't believe it. He thought Harding was taking the mickey out of his impediment. Angrily, he stuttered back his reply. Now it was Love's turn to be furious, thinking that Harding was taking the mickey out of him. Tempers flared as the interview progressed through several stuttered questions and answers. Then the two men were on their feet, ready to fight each other. It was only the swift intervention of a quick-thinking public relations man that stopped them. He realised the misunderstanding, got between them and explained that no-one was taking the mickey out of anyone. Love and Harding stared at each other, then collapsed with laughter. It was the start of a long friendship…

★ ★ ★

Dicky Maegle, a star player for Rice University football team, was on his way to make an impressive 95-yard touchdown in the 1954 Dallas Cotton Bowl when he was floored by a flying tackle. The man who brought him down was Alabama full back Tommy Lewis – and as soon as he made the tackle he regretted it. You see, at the time, Lewis was a substitute. He was sitting on the bench when Maegle ran past him on the sidelines and Lewis's instinct got the better of him. The crowd of 75,000 went silent as Lewis shambled back, trying to look as if nothing had happened. As Maegle dusted himself off, the referee picked up the ball and personally carried it the rest of the way to the Alabama touchdown – where it would eventually have ended up.

After the game Lewis apologised to Maegle and told the press, 'I kept telling myself, "I didn't do it. I didn't do it." But I knew I did! I don't think I'll ever get over it.'

Ironically, in the game Maegle broke all records for scoring in the history of the Bowl, but it was Lewis whose name was on the nation's lips.

★ ★ ★

In 1968, the third division football match between Plymouth Argyle and Barrow was settled by a single goal – sensationally scored by the referee, Ivan Robinson! With ten minutes left to play, Barrow were awarded a corner. The ball came into the area and was cleared away by a Plymouth defender as far as Barrow forward George McLean. He took a shot but

> The pace of the match is really accelerating, by which I mean it's getting faster all the time.
> – David Coleman

the ball headed well wide of the goal, towards where the referee was standing 12 yards from the goalmouth. The ref saw it coming and jumped to avoid the ball, but it deflected off his foot and tucked itself neatly between the keeper and the post. The red-faced referee had no choice but to award himself – and Barrow – the goal.

> ' Ah! Isn't that nice, the wife of the Cambridge president is kissing the cox of the Oxford crew. '
> – Harry Carpenter, commentating on the 1977 Boat Race

* * *

Who could blame American commentator Connie Desmond when he collapsed in fits of laughter during a 1951 National Invitational Basketball Match at Madison Square Garden? It all happened because of the name of one of the players – North Carolina star Bernie Yurin. It's pronounced exactly as you think. Desmond's co-commentator, Marty Glickman, just couldn't stop himself saying things like, 'Yurin's shot has been blocked', 'Look at Yurin dribbling' and 'I've never seen Yurin look so hot'.

* * *

Cricket fans everywhere wanted to see West Indian cricketer Clive Lloyd do well in his last professional game, played appropriately enough at Lord's. He received a standing ovation as he walked from the pavilion to the wicket – and another one on his way back. Unfortunately there wasn't long between the two, since Clive was out for a duck.

* * *

One athlete who took his sport perhaps a little too seriously was the Japanese marathon runner Kokichi Tsuburaya. Running in front of his home crowd at the 1964 Tokyo Olympics, he managed a creditable third place but this was not good enough for him. After the Games he resumed training but soon fell into a deep depression. Nine months before the 1968 Mexico Olympics he committed hara-kiri, ritual suicide, leaving behind a note in which he apologised for failing his country.

★ ★ ★

A West German soccer star by the name of Karl-Heinz Granitza was imported to America to add a touch of class to the Chicago Sting soccer team. Granitza found the transition very difficult, primarily because he couldn't speak one word of English. This led to numerous confusions and misunderstandings – but none more serious than on the day his team flew out of Chicago's O'Hare Airport for an away fixture. Granitza arrived separately, and couldn't make head nor tail of the destination boards, signs or announcements in the airport. He ended up boarding entirely the wrong flight and it wasn't until the plane started to taxi out that he realised something was up. There were no other members of his team on the flight for a start. Granitza panicked, jumped up and started yelling in German for the plane to stop and let him off. Pandemonium broke out, as people started screaming and running about the aircraft in all directions. Unable to understand what Granitza was saying, they had assumed he was trying to hijack the aircraft!

> ❛ It's a very well-run outfit from Monday to Friday. It's Saturdays we've got a problem with. ❜
> – Lawrie McMenemy (on Southampton)

★　★　★

When world heavyweight contender Floyd Patterson took on
Sonny Liston in 1962 he must have known he was in for a
beating. Before the match he'd bought a disguise and, after his
humiliating defeat in just 126 seconds, he slipped past the
spectators in his false beard and glasses.

★　★　★

The Plainfield Teachers were the American football sensation of
1941, and sports reporters were falling over themselves to write
feature articles about them. Sports fans the length and breadth of
America followed their games. The only problem was, they didn't
exist.

    The Plainfield Teachers were the invention of a bored Wall
Street stockbroker called Morris Newburger. He was fed up with
reading sports reports about what he considered to be
insignificant teams from the back of beyond and so decided to
create his own fictitious side. He rang up the *New York Herald
Tribune* and gave them a report on the Teachers' 20–0 thrashing
of 'the Beacon Institute'. The *Tribune* took him seriously and
promised to publish. This gave Newburger even more confidence
and he went on to supply the same hoax sports report to the *New
York Times*, the Associated Press and the United Press. Soon,
America was following the
Teachers as they battled
their way through the
entirely imaginary
Blackboard Bowl
Championship, thrilling
to the exploits of the
team's hero, Johnny

> I left because of illness
> and fatigue. The fans
> were sick and tired of me.
> – John Ralston (ex-coach, the
> Denver Broncos)

Cheung, 'The Celestial Comet', who was a 212-pound 'full-blooded' Chinese American, and the team's maverick manager, Ralph 'Hurry Up' Hoblitzel, inventor of the unique 'W' formation. Herb Allen of the *New York Post* managed somehow to write an entire feature article on Johnny Cheung, despite the fact that he didn't exist. Eventually, *Time* magazine managed to work out the hoax and a great many sports commentators of the day ended up with a lot of egg on their faces.

★　★　★

Cricketers Ian Botham and Derek Randall would often try and outdo each other playing pranks when they were on tour. The two of them were once 'off duty' in Adelaide when Botham bet Randall £10 that he wouldn't swap clothes with a girl they met in a bar. Randall accepted and was soon wearing her mini-skirt. Botham then bet him a further £5 that he wouldn't go out in the street dressed like that. Randall was game for a laugh and willingly accepted. However, he went one further by standing on the kerb, propositioning car drivers.

It wasn't long before he was picked up by a burly driver, at which point the English cricketer had to explain who he really was. However, he didn't believe Randall's story, and thought the 'girl' he'd picked up was just playing hard to get. After a punch-up Randall managed to escape from the car with his reputation (or what was left of it) intact.

★　★　★

Oxbarn Social Club from Wolverhampton played in a local Sunday football league, and on a tour of Germany in 1973, the club decided to get some practice in. Arrangements were made to play a local German team. However, Oxbarn's club secretary realised something was wrong when they turned up to play the match. Instead of a public recreation ground they arrived at a luxury stadium. It turned out that their opponents were the German first division team SVW Mainz, who themselves were expecting to play Wolverhampton Wanderers, then a top team.

The error was realised but the match went ahead anyway. Oxbarn Social Club were grateful for the experience they gained from playing a top-class European team. Even though they lost 21–0.

★　　★　　★

Keen athletes will practise anywhere, and none were more keen than three athletes representing Mozambique in the 1991 World Student Games in Sheffield. They were delighted to find a nice stretch of straight road to run on which was close to their accommodation. Their practice sessions were soon brought to a halt, though, when they were arrested by police and charged with running on the M1.

✶   ✶   ✶

The Minnesota Vikings American football team would love to find out who had a grudge against them and altered their usual office recorded message in 1991. Callers on hold were greeted by the new message, 'Thank you for calling the most rotten, stinking team in the history of man. That's right. You have reached the Minnesota Vikings.'

✶   ✶   ✶

George Chuvalo, the Canadian heavyweight boxing champion, fought George Foreman in August 1970. Always the underdog, the fight was soon going against the Canadian champ. There were cuts above his eyes, he was dribbling blood from his mouth, he had a glazed look and was stumbling about as he took punch after punch.

Just when it looked like he was going to be KO'd, Chuvalo's wife decided she wasn't going to take her husband's punishment lying down (even though he was about to). Twice she tried to clamber over the ropes and get in the ring to stop the fight and twice she was restrained by officials. To her relief the contest was stopped in the third round. It turned out that intervening in her husband's bouts wasn't anything new. She'd done the same thing in a previous fight against Joe Frazier, before telling her husband to give up boxing for good. 'He won't use his head,' she complained. 'I've tried again and again to get him to quit.' This time she was successful.

> ‘ Martin Schanche's car is absolutely unique, except for the one behind it, which is identical! ’
> – Murray Walker

✱   ✱   ✱

Apparently President Clinton is a big fan of Sumo wrestling –
which got him into a spot of diplomatic hot water with the
ex German Chancellor Helmut Kohl. 'I was thinking of you
last night, Helmut, because I watched the Sumo wrestling on
television,' he once told the 280-pound Kohl, who was reportedly
not amused…

✱   ✱   ✱

This feels like telling tales but I'm sure he won't mind. Jimmy Hill
was once preparing for an interview with rugby player Nigel
Starmer-Smith. Since it was the sort of name that can give
presenters problems, Jimmy repeated the name over and over
again to be sure he got it right on air. The live interview started
and Jimmy got the name of the player spot on. Unfortunately, he
then went on to say that Starmer-Smith 'had seven craps as scum
half for England'.

✱   ✱   ✱

In February 1936, the Football League descended into chaos after
deciding to declare war on the football pools companies who
they thought brought a disreputable element into the sport. They
decided to wreck the pools companies' business by refusing to
publish fixture lists. Posters promoting forthcoming matches
appeared saying things like 'Sheffield Wednesday vs ?' The clubs
themselves, of course, got mightily confused.
Some failed to turn up for
matches. Others went to the
wrong grounds or turned up
for away fixtures when they
were meant to be playing at

> ❝ Viv Anderson had
> pissed a fatness test.
> – Commentator John Helm ❞

home. They could have found out who and where they were meant to be playing, however, simply by reading the pools coupons! Throughout it all, the pools companies still managed somehow to get the full facts on fixtures and, ironically, published the most accurate lists available anywhere! The League soon gave up…and the pools have been with us ever since.

★ ★ ★

The Harlem Globetrotters came to London in the early 1960s and entranced thousands of spectators with their unbelievable wizardry and amazing ball control. Fulham goalkeeper Tony Macedo was so captivated by the antics of Meadowlark Lemon and his team that he decided to adopt a few of their tricks in Fulham's next match against Spurs at Craven Cottage.

During the match he decided to bounce the ball around his goalmouth, basketball style (this was in the days before the current four-step rule for goalkeepers). The crowd went wild, so he did it again. Unfortunately the ball slipped from his grasp and an unmarked Jimmy Greaves promptly put it into the net.

★ ★ ★

The American author Jim Fixx pioneered better health through jogging and turned the craze into an industry in the 1970s. He wrote the best-selling *The Complete Book of Running* in 1977 and prided himself on being able to run ten miles each day, claiming that 'research has shown that with endurance training such as running, the heart becomes a distinctly more efficient instrument'. He died in July 1984 while out jogging – from a massive heart attack.

★ ★ ★

If this story hadn't appeared in the pages of the venerable *Times* itself, I'm not sure I would have believed a word of it! Emilio Tarra was a crew member on an America's Cup yacht. He was taking some shore leave in Australia, driving between Perth and Adelaide, when a kangaroo suddenly jumped out in front of his car. There was no way he could miss it and the kangaroo struck his bumper with a sickening bang. Emilio stopped, climbed out and evaluated the situation, looking down at the dead 'roo in front of his car. Then, of course, he did what we'd all do in such a situation. He decided to prop the 'roo up on the bonnet, dress it up in his yachting blazer and take a souvenir photograph. As he stepped back to frame his photograph, the kangaroo started to stir. It had only been stunned by the impact. With a flick of its powerful tail, the kangaroo decked Emilio and then hopped away into the bush again – still wearing Emilio's yachting blazer. It was only when Emilio got back into his car that he realised the blazer contained his passport, 16 credit cards and 2,000 Australian dollars in cash!

★   ★   ★

In 1979, Washington golf pro Ron Coleman decided to promote a new line in sports bras in his club shop. He wanted to do this by holding a golf tournament just for women. Nothing wrong with that you might think. Except that Ron wanted to separate contestants not by their handicap but by their bust size. As soon as the contest was announced the club was besieged by women's groups who complained it was sexist, demeaning and discriminatory. Not surprisingly it was banned and Ron had to apologise to all concerned for his gigantic boob.

★   ★   ★

Everyone remembers Eddie 'The Eagle' Edwards with affection. Once described as 'Mr Magoo on skis', as well as leaping into last place in the 1988 Calgary Winter Olympics, he also has the distinction of being beaten by his own helmet. This happened while he was training for the Calgary Olympics in Kanersteg in Switzerland. At the time, Eddie's lack of funding meant that his crash helmet was pitifully old and held in place only by string. Eddie pushed himself off for the 90-metre jump, but at the point of take-off the string snapped and he and his helmet parted company. Eddie managed to jump 54 metres – but the helmet managed 93 metres.

When it came to the event itself Eddie was terrified but still persevered. 'When I looked from the top of the jump,' he said afterwards, 'I was so frightened that my bum shrivelled up like a prune.'

★　★　★

After England's 2–0 win against Tunisia in the 1998 World Cup this year, coach Glenn Hoddle and the first goalscorer Alan Shearer were interviewed on TV. But when the interview was broadcast Hoddle remained in shot all the time, with Shearer's comments being delivered 'off camera'. No explanation was given but I can now reveal what happened.

During the interview, Alan was standing in front of a long banner that read 'Marseilles', where the game took place. Unfortunately, he was standing in front of the 'M' and all you would have seen on your TV screen were Alan and the second, third, fourth and fifth letters…

> The World Cup. Truly an international event.
> – John Motson

CHAPTER 3

The Boy's a Natural

'There's no skill involved. Just go up there and swing at the ball'
– *Joe DiMaggio's tip for playing better baseball*

The spectators at the 1950 Empire Games were confused at the technique adopted by South African hurdler Tom Avery. In the final of the 120-yard hurdles he seemed to leap over each hurdle holding his shorts up by the waist. The reason was simple: the button fastening his shorts had popped off as soon as he started running. Holding his shorts up in this way without breaking his stride enabled him to hide his embarrassment – and avoid tripping over at the same time. Despite this handicap Avery still managed to win the bronze medal.

★　★　★

A new car was offered as the prize for hitting a hole in one at a tournament held in South Dakota in 1991, so imagine DeAun West's excitement when she hit a hole in one on the second hole. Sorry, the officials said, we meant a hole in one at the twelfth hole. DeAun then hit her second hole in one of the day at the twelfth – and went home with the car!

★   ★   ★

One of the strangest goals in football history was scored by
'Mighty Atom' Patsy Gallagher at the Scottish FA Cup Final in
1925. The diminutive Celtic player had made an exceptional run
from inside his own half, but got tangled up with Dundee
defenders before falling over in the penalty area. Gripping the
ball between both feet, he then did an amazing somersault over
the line and into the back of the net, taking the ball with him. It
took several minutes to disentangle Gallagher from the netting –
but the goal stood.

★   ★   ★

Many American presidents have come from impressive sporting
backgrounds. Hard as it is to imagine, Abraham Lincoln was
famed as a wrestler. According to someone who knew him in his
youth, he could 'outrun, whip or throw any man in the county'.
He was also an excellent swimmer, a local handball champion
and a big fan of ten-pin bowling, as was Harry S Truman, who
had a bowling alley installed in the White House basement
during his term as president.

★   ★   ★

Cuban President Fidel Castro played baseball for assorted minor
league teams in the US and even had a trial with the Washington
Senators baseball team. He didn't get picked, but went on to put
his swimming prowess to good use in films with the aquatic
Hollywood star Esther Williams!

★   ★   ★

The Russian wrestler and weightlifter George Hackenschmidt was obsessed with physical fitness and once lifted a milkman's horse on to his shoulders and carried it about. When he was eighty-five he could (and would) jump 50 times consecutively over the back of a chair.

* * *

In 1805, the British heavyweight boxing champion, Henry Pierce, went to visit one of his friends unfortunate enough to be locked up in London's debtors' jail. While he was there, the other prisoners begged him to put on an exhibition bout for them and poor John Gully, an apprentice butcher's boy, was pushed forward from the ranks of the prisoners to spar with the champion. Incredibly, Gully wiped the floor with Pierce in double quick time! News of the champion's humiliating defeat reached the outside world and a wealthy sportsman agreed to pay off Gully's debts to free him and then to sponsor him in the outside world. It proved to be a shrewd investment, as the young butcher's boy went on to become the heavyweight champion of the world! From abject debt and poverty, Gully went on to amass a personal fortune. He bought a string of racehorses, two of which won the Derby, while others won the Oaks and St Leger. Gully even became a Member of Parliament and, when he died in 1863, he was officially a millionaire.

Most people know that Spanish crooner Julio Iglesias used to play in goal for Real Madrid. Nobel prize winning writer Albert Camus was also a goalie, for the Algerian team Oran. But Polish goalie Karol Wojtyla had a much stranger career change after hanging up his boots – he became Pope John Paul II.

By 1904, the British Grand National had achieved such prestige that horses from around the world were being entered for it. In South Africa, a thoroughbred horse called Moifaa was put aboard a ship for England and the National – only to sail headlong into one of the worst storms ever recorded in the area. The ship floundered and Moifaa was pitched off the boat into the raging seas. Incredibly, the horse swam over 100 miles through the storm and reached the South African coast and safety.

Did you know?

Clifford 'Tippy' Gray, the songwriter who wrote 'If You Were the Only Girl in the World', won an Olympic gold in both the 1928 and 1932 four-man bobsled event.

Instead of giving him a well-deserved rest, his owners decided to ship Moifaa back out again on the next suitable boat for England. Long before the horse reached these shores, news of his incredible swim had reached the English gambling fraternity. They thought Moifaa would be

> **Did you know?**
>
> Comedian Eddie Large was once offered a trial by Manchester City, and did you know that Sir David Frost turned down a trial with Nottingham Forest FC?

in no state to run the National and gave him unflattering odds of 25–1. Most thought he'd not even finish after all he'd been through. They completely failed to recognise the guts and sheer stamina the horse had shown to survive – and it was a costly mistake, as Moifaa romped home the easy winner of the race.

★   ★   ★

New York City hosts the annual Backward Mile Race. Contestants celebrate the spirit of backwardness by running forwards, but looking backwards. When does it take place? Every April Fool's Day, of course.

Runner Donald Davis did it the harder way. He ran the whole 1982 Honolulu marathon backwards in a very commendable time of 4 hours 20 minutes. The same year, a 27-year-old athlete called Anthony 'Scott' Weiland ran the Detroit marathon backwards in 4 hours, 7 minutes and 54 seconds. But that's nothing compared to the record set by Plennie Wingo who ran backwards from Santa Monica, California to Istanbul, Turkey in 1931. It took him six months to cover the 8,000 miles.

★   ★   ★

Tension was mounting in the 1997 Gateshead football match between the Portland Arms pub team and their bitter rivals from the Coach and Horses. The score was 4–4 with a minute left on the clock. Watching from the sideline, no-one felt the tension more than Nipper, a seven-month-old Staffordshire Terrier belonging to Portland Arms captain Steve Wraith. Unable to just stand there and do nothing, Nipper frantically wriggled free of his leash and bounded onto the pitch. He grabbed the ball from under the feet of the opposing centre half and headed off towards goal with it. Three defenders moved to intercept Nipper, but with a dazzling combination of fancy paw-work, body swerves and the odd threatening growl, he shrugged them off. Then with a flick of his neck, he neatly centred for striker Gary Roberts to put the ball past the astounded Coach and Horses goalie!

As you might expect, every head on the pitch turned to look at the referee. There was a pause, and then he pointed to the centre spot. It was a goal! The match ended 5–4, and Nipper joined his team in a lap of honour around the pitch afterwards!

★　★　★

Someone in a pub once unwittingly challenged Joe Davis to a snooker match, unaware that the man had been world billiard champion four times, world snooker champion fifteen times and, in 1955, had scored the world's first-ever maximum snooker break of 147. Not surprisingly, Davis completely wiped the floor with his opponent, who said, 'Blimey, you must know Joe Davis!' Joe replied, 'Not very well – but I do sleep with his wife!'

Did you know?

The great snooker player Joe Davis only had one eye.

✦   ✦   ✦

Norman Wisdom was Army boxing champion in 1932! Other people you may not have realised were keen boxers include US President Teddy Roosevelt, Lord Byron, Berry Gordy (the founder of Motown Records), inventor of the steam locomotive George Stephenson, Pope John Paul II, Eamonn Andrews, Kris Kristofferson, the singer Terence Trent D'Arby, Idi Amin (Ugandan heavyweight champion for nine years), Bob Hope, Arthur Mullard, Billy Joel, Chris Isaak, John Fashanu, Jack Palance and Ernest Hemingway.

✦   ✦   ✦

Back in the late 1960s, a small-time teenage crook was going from car to car in a quiet Chicago residential road looking for a vehicle to steal. He found one he particularly liked and although it was locked, he tried to force the doors. The commotion was heard by the car's owner, a middle-aged man who came rushing out of his house, yelling at the thief.

Having nearly a forty-year age advantage on his pursuer, the young thief wasn't particularly worried about being caught and slowly put away his tools and jogged away from the scene of the crime. To his dismay, the senior citizen chasing him didn't show any signs of giving up, let alone getting tired. In fact, no matter how fast the thief ran, his pursuer seemed to be gaining, and it wasn't long before he'd caught up

Did you know?

Dennis Weaver, better known as 1970s TV cowboy cop McCloud, came sixth in the 1948 US Olympic Decathlon trials.

with him, holding the out-of-breath crook until police arrived.

They recognised the intended victim and told the thief who it was. In between gasping for breath he told them, 'I've always been a loser. Only me would try and rob Jesse Owens.'

Incidentally, Jesse Owens wasn't really called Jesse Owens. He was actually called James Cleveland Owens but on his first day at elementary school a teacher asked him his name. The shy little boy replied 'Jay Cee Owens' in his slow Southern accent and the teacher misheard it as 'Jesse'. The name stuck.

★　★　★

Hermanus Brockmann was coxswain for the Dutch crew in the coxed-pairs event at the 1900 Paris Olympics. They reached the finals but the team manager was concerned that Brockmann was too heavy. What they needed, he concluded, was someone who was first and foremost very light – an understanding of how to actually steer the boat was secondary. Given this objective, the team recruited a seven-year-old Parisian boy who was hanging around their boat.

> **Did you know?**
>
> World-famous child care expert Dr Benjamin Spock was a member of the US rowing team in the 1924 Paris Olympics.

His name is lost in history and the legality of this substitution is unclear but he helped the Dutch crew to victory, in the process becoming the youngest-ever Olympic gold medallist.

★　★　★

Pint-sized Felix Carvajal had never shown the slightest interest in running so when, in 1904, the Cuban postman announced to his family and work colleagues that he intended to win the Olympic marathon event, they thought he'd gone crazy. So did the people gathered in the public square in Havana, where Felix decided to raise the money he needed to go to the Olympics by racing around and around in circles and begging for contributions. Felix worked tirelessly for weeks, finally begging enough for his fare to the Games, which were being held in St Louis.

Arriving by boat at New Orleans, which was then a very wild and disreputable town, the naïve little postman soon fell foul of professional card sharks, who cheated him out of every penny he possessed. It looked like Felix's dream was over. He was broke and friendless in a strange town – but he wasn't beaten yet. Felix gritted his teeth and decided he'd run the 700 miles to the Games. So he did, begging food from farmhouses along the way until he arrived at St Louis.

Felix turned up at the starting line for the marathon, exhausted, hungry and wearing heavy walking boots and a long-sleeved shirt and trousers – the only clothes he had. A fellow competitor felt sorry for him and snipped off the arms and legs of his clothes so he didn't look too out of place. As the competitors set off, it was a

Did you know?

Bill Nankeville, who competed in the 1948 London Olympics 1500 metres, is Bobby Davro's father.

Did you know?

★ Paul Newman came second in the 1979 Le Mans 24 hour race. (Yes, *the* Paul Newman.)

★ Singer Johnny Mathis used to be a world-rated high jumper.

★ What do Marcel Marceau, Neil Diamond, JP Donleavy and Anita Harris all have in common? They're all accomplished fencers.

scorching hot day and the temperature kept on rising until it reached 90 degrees. The little Cuban soon set a blistering pace and many competitors dropped away behind him. Then his hunger got the better of him and he stopped off in an apple orchard for a quick bite – which turned into a rather long stay. In fact, Felix ate so many apples that he got stomach cramp and had to lie down for a while, allowing the others to catch up and overtake him.

Of the 31 runners who set off, only 14 finished, including the valiant little Cuban. Sadly, he didn't win after all he'd been through. He didn't even get a medal, coming fourth, but he still carved himself a place in the Olympic Hall of Fame as the incredible 'Felix the Fourth'.

★ ★ ★

Irving Baxter, the American and Olympic pole vault champion, arrived at the 1900 Paris Games without his pole, after it had been lost en route. His competitors saw this was their chance to beat him and refused to lend him their poles. Baxter was so angry that he uprooted a flagpole and used that instead, eventually winning the title with a vault of 10 feet 10 inches.

★ ★ ★

Sports commentators have to be quick-witted, and able to react to anything that happens on the field. In the US a few years ago, Don Meredith was reporting on a particularly boring football game when the camera zoomed in on a fan dozing in his seat. Suddenly the man woke up, saw the camera looking at him and gave Don (and his millions of viewers) the middle-finger salute. Without pausing Don just said, 'And this fan's trying to tell us that he thinks his team is number one!'

On another occasion, American football player Ronnie Lewis of Louisiana State University gave two middle-fingered salutes to a jeering crowd. The commentator quickly explained that the player was signalling to the spectators that his team was eleventh in the league (which they were).

CHAPTER 4

Sports Mad

'Ha ha! We are the best in the world!
We have beaten England! Lord Nelson, Lord
Beaverbrook, Sir Winston Churchill, Sir Anthony
Eden, Clement Attlee, Henry Cooper, Lady Diana –
we have beaten them all! Maggie Thatcher, can you
hear me? Maggie Thatcher, your boys took a
hell of a beating! Norway have beaten
England at football!'
– *A rather excited Norwegian radio commentator*
describing England's 1981 2–1 defeat by Norway
during the World Cup qualifiers

A group of football fans from the Bolivian village of Ixiamas were celebrating their national team's win over Uruguay in the traditional way of throwing firecrackers. They were so wrapped up in their jubilation that they failed to realise the firecrackers had set their houses' thatched roofs alight, burning virtually the entire village to the ground.

★　★　★

Newly-wed Ken Overlin and his best man Spike Webb were
punching seven bells out of each other just minutes after Ken's
wedding to his fiancée Madeline Smith. It was all right though;
Ken was a professional boxer (later to become world
middleweight champion) and the best man was his opponent.
They fought in Virginia in 1927, after Ken and Madeline had
received special permission to get married in the boxing ring.
The bride wore a traditional white dress while Ken, so he didn't
waste time before his bout, wore his boxing shorts and ring
shoes.

★　★　★

Who's the number-one sports fan in the world? During his
presidency, Richard Nixon thought he was, and was forever
telling everyone. He was so sports mad that he even used football
terms as code words for US activities in Vietnam. 'Operation
Linebacker' was the code name for mining Hanoi's harbours and
the Vietnam peace negotiations were known as 'Quarterback'.

But it was his interference in everyday sport that really annoyed the professionals. He was watching the Washington Redskins play San Francisco in 1972 when he phoned the Redskins' coach George Allen from the Oval Office to offer his advice. He told

> I'm a great fan of baseball. I watch a lot of games on the radio.
> – US President Gerald Ford

him to use a particular flanking move that he guaranteed would work. Not wanting to insult the President, Allen followed Nixon's advice. It was a disaster and his team lost 24–20.

Another time he rang the coach of the Miami Dolphins, Don Shula, at 1.30 am to tell him a particular play. Shula told reporters that at first he thought it was some nut calling, but he followed Nixon's advice anyway. It failed.

★ ★ ★

It was a real basketball grudge match between the Universities of Wichita and Detroit in 1956. The spectators were drunk and unruly, players were tense and the officials, Alex George and Cliff Ogden, were trying their best to calm the atmosphere.

It wasn't easy. Detroit were losing by one point with four seconds to go and the home team, Wichita, were looking forward to a famous victory. In the last second of the match a Detroit player tried a desperate shot which would have worked – if the hoop hadn't been covered by the coat of a Wichita fan, who'd dropped it from the balcony. The ball hit the coat just before the final buzzer sounded. The basketball court went silent. All eyes were on the two officials. George told his partner, 'It's 120 feet to the dressing room and I'm not going to call anything until we both get to the door.' Both officials then walked off the court and just before he bolted their dressing room door, George called the shot a basket – the winning shot for the visitors.

They didn't leave the sanctuary of their dressing room for some hours after the match.

★　★　★

Most football fans show their disapproval of the ref by calling him every name under the sun. This is usually enough to vent their anger – but not in Peru. Referee Felipe Compinez awarded a controversial penalty during a local cup competition but was stoned to death by angry fans who stormed the pitch after a goal was scored.

★　★　★

The English actor Trevor Howard was such a cricket fan that he had a clause in all his movie contracts stating that he would not be required for filming during any Test match played at Lord's.

★　★　★

Lots of football fans attend every home game their club plays, but how many manage it after their death? It happened to a supporter of the Spanish side Real Betis. His dying wishes were to be cremated, and for his ashes to be taken by his son to every home game until his season ticket ran out. Sure enough, the week after the funeral, the son took his dad's ashes in an old jam jar to the Benito Villemarin stadium, placing them carefully on his seat.

★　★　★

The Danish tennis player Torben Ulrich walked off court and forfeited the game during a vital match at Wimbledon just so he could watch the 1966 World Cup Final on TV.

★ ★ ★

The rather aptly named greyhound 'Mental's Only Hope' set a new sporting record at Wimbledon Stadium on 29 March 1961 when he turned the traditional sprinting race into a marathon. Perhaps ashamed of coming last in his race, 'Mental' kept on running round and round the track, furiously weaving and dodging around the increasingly perplexed owners and officials trying to catch him. No-one's sure how many laps he ran, but he kept going for a record 30 minutes and 29 seconds before stopping!

★ ★ ★

Mr Dennis Lovesey lived near a cricket ground at Holton-Le-Clay but got so fed up with spectators blocking the access to his house with their cars that in 1985 he drove his lorry on to the middle of the pitch and refused to move it. The match, against Barton-on-Humber, had to be stopped while officials appealed for those drivers blocking Mr Lovesey's road to move.

* * *

Football can arouse such strong passions even amongst the most unlikely of people. Sister Collette Duveen, a nun belonging to the Order of Merciful Sisters, found herself under arrest for kicking in the teeth of a burly truck driver who had shouted 'Hooray!' when Holland scored their only goal against Argentina in the 1978 World Cup Final.

* * *

In 1982 an airliner prepared for an emergency landing after it suddenly developed long and violent vibrations. Eventually the cause was traced to a super-keen jogger who had locked himself in the toilet so he could do an hour's running on the spot.

* * *

The 1938 Italian World Cup Final team received a personal telegram from Il Duce Benito Mussolini. It read 'Win or die.' Almost as harsh, perhaps, was the message on the huge banner at Rome airport awaiting the Italian national side after being knocked out of the 1966 World Cup. It read: 'Italy vomits on you.'

In the 1980s the President of Liberia personally told the African Cup team that, if they let their country down, they would all face the firing squad! Quite understandably, tension ran rather high in their match against The Gambia. It ended in a goalless draw and the Liberian team, nicknamed the 'Lone Stars', were left pondering whether it was worth even taking a bath

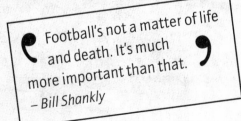

Football's not a matter of life and death. It's much more important than that.
– Bill Shankly

or not. However, the Liberian President decided they had done
enough and commuted their death sentences.

★　★　★

In February 1996 four golfers were engrossed in a match at the
Boca Raton municipal golf course in Florida. They were so
caught up in the game that they failed to notice something
heading straight towards them on one of the greens – a Piper
Aero light aircraft in the middle of making an emergency landing
due to engine problems. The student pilot made a safe landing
but the golfers were totally oblivious – so much so that the
instructor, Scott Slinko, had to veer the plane away from them,
clipping a palm tree in the process. He told reporters that
'Everything would have been okay if those damn golfers would
have moved out of the way. We were coming down and they
weren't moving, so I went for the tree.'

In their defence Irv Brown, one of the four golfers, claimed they were just following sage advice from one of golf's greats: 'Concentration – that's the name of the game. That's what Jack Nicklaus said, and we were concentrating.'

★　★　★

All golfers have their off days, but Richard Arntzen of Ohio took one particular game to heart. After playing badly he went berserk with his nine iron, destroying an electric golf cart and violently beating his two opponents and a policeman who was called to the scene. Mr Arntzen was finally restrained with the help of tear gas. He later apologised to the authorities and told them, 'You know how it is. I had a bad round.'

★　★　★

A recent study commissioned by the Japanese Ministry of Health showed that golf is one of the most dangerous sports in the country in terms of killing men over 60 years old. These findings were endorsed by Doctor Keizo Kogure who estimates that internationally nearly 5,000 men die on golf courses each year, the majority as a result of stress caused by the game's competitiveness in Japan. His findings were published in his own book, *How To Die Early By Playing Golf*.

★　★　★

American Jay Helgerson must have been one of the most fanatical runners in the world. In 1979 he ran a marathon each week except one when he got bored and did two in one weekend.

Following in his footsteps was New Yorker Mike Kasser. He ran the 1983 London Marathon in 2 hours 56 minutes 30 seconds, then dashed to Heathrow Airport where he flew by Concorde to compete in the Boston marathon the next day, achieving a very respectable 3 hours 8 minutes.

★ ★ ★

Mary Queen of Scots was one of the world's first recorded golf fanatics. She was so dedicated to the game that two days after the death of her husband Darnley she was playing golf in the grounds of her residence Seton House. (Mary was also a keen billiards player and was inconsolable when she had her table confiscated after her arrest on the orders of Elizabeth I.)

★ ★ ★

A football match that led to a war took place in South America in June 1969. It was a three-leg World Cup qualifier between bitter rivals El Salvador and neighbours Honduras. As an indication of the fervour that was to follow, Amelia Bolanios, an El Salvador fan, shot herself at the first leg's final whistle as she couldn't bear the shame the 1–0 defeat brought to her country.

In the second leg the El Salvador fans were whipped into a frenzy when, during the national anthems, the Honduran flag was ceremonially burned. In the end the tense match was won 3–0 by El Salvador. After the match, violence gripped the country, and visiting Honduran fans were violently attacked. Two were killed and this led to the border between the two countries being closed.

> Football is like nuclear warfare. There are no winners, just survivors.
> – Frank Gifford, former pro footballer player and sportscaster

By the third and final leg both countries had broken off diplomatic relations. The game was played in neutral Mexico City and El Salvador won 3–2, a late penalty deciding the game. Back home, rival fans rioted through both capital cities and the match was fought again, this time on the streets. A week after the game, war broke out between the two nations. This lasted for four days and resulted in the destruction of oil refineries and the deaths of 2,000 troops.

> You give 100 per cent in the first half of the game, and if that isn't enough, in the second half you give what's left.
> —Yogi Berra

★　★　★

There's no more bitter rivalry than that between the fans of Newcastle United and Sunderland. Newcastle supporters working for the Post Office were once reprimanded for defacing letters and packages destined for Sunderland with slogans like 'Failures', 'Utter Cr*p' – and worse.

Getting their own back, Sunderland supporters boycotted Sugar Puffs because Kevin Keegan, the then Newcastle manager, appeared in their commercial alongside the Honey Monster. The boycott got local publicity and Sugar Puff sales in Sunderland plummeted.

★　★　★

Riddick Bowe lost his WBA heavyweight title due to distraction in the ring – or at least that's what he claimed after his November 1993 fight with Evander Holyfield. The bout took place at the Caesar's Palace Outdoor Stadium and about 70 seconds into round seven an unexpected visitor dropped in to see the fighters – 30-year-old boxing fan and sky diver James 'Windy' Miller, who

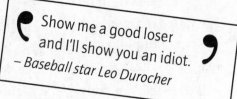

Show me a good loser and I'll show you an idiot.
– Baseball star Leo Durocher

parachuted into the ring. Nicknamed 'The Fan Man' because of the large petrol-drive rotor used to control his descent, Miller got entangled in the ropes and was immediately beaten up by Bowe's entourage before being arrested by police and dragged away. Bowe's wife Judy fainted in the fracas and the fight was delayed for 21 minutes while both astonished boxers waited in the ring.

After his defeat Bowe told reporters, 'I had Holyfield right where I wanted him. His back was bothering him, his legs were tired and I think he was ready to quit. If "Fan Man" hadn't come in, I'd have knocked him out in that round or in the next.'

In the US, nothing interferes with a TV network's scheduling, not even when the New York Jets were leading the Oakland Raiders in a nail-biting match to determine who would win the Western Division title in 1968.

NBC were televising the game live but had the film *Heidi* lined up for 7 pm. At 6.50 pm the match was tied 29–29 and viewers were on the edge of their seats. At 6.58pm New York were leading 32–29. Seconds before 7 pm the Raiders were on the offensive. Then the game was interrupted by *Heidi*. Viewers went berserk and so many called NBC to complain that the switchboard blew. What they didn't see was Oakland score two last-minute touchdowns to win the game. The local news that night included this report: 'The result of tonight's football game was the Jets, 32, Oakland, 43 – and Heidi married the goat herder.'

✦ ✦ ✦

Football can sometimes arouse strong and dangerous passions. In July 1982 a German fan wanted to watch the national side in a vital World Cup game while his wife wanted to watch the feature film, *For Whom The Bells Toll*. They argued back and forth about who should watch what – and why. Eventually the football fan hit upon a solution to the problem of only having one TV in the house – he threw his wife through the window.

Retired Yugoslavian policeman Marinko Janevski was a real football fanatic who would let nothing get in the way of watching the Yugoslavian equivalent of *Match of the Day*, not even when his wife turned off the TV to get his attention. Marinko calmly strangled her, turned the set back on and carried on watching. At his trial in 1982 he was found guilty of manslaughter. The judge accepted his partial defence of 'I always get excited when I watch football.'

★ ★ ★

British walker Don Thompson prepared himself for the
overbearing heat of the 1960 Rome Olympics by training for a
year in his bathroom, with the doors and windows sealed, the
central heating turned up to maximum and surrounded by
boiling kettles. It did the trick and he returned home with a gold
medal – and a gas bill of nearly £10,000.

CHAPTER 5

Rules are Made to be Broken

'If it moves you kick it; if it doesn't move,
you kick it 'til it does.'
– *Phil Woosnam (ex-Welsh international)*
teaching the basics of soccer to Americans

Legendary comedians Harpo Marx and George Burns were once
playing golf together at the elite Hillcrest Golf Club. As the
temperature soared, both men took their shirts off. It was only a
matter of moments before an immaculately dressed official
appeared. 'The club's written rules clearly state players must keep
their shirts on,' he told them. Burns and Marx dutifully put their
shirts on and the official strode off satisfied. However, some
instinct made him turn to look back – to see the two comedians
now taking their trousers off instead. He rushed back to
remonstrate with them. 'Are there any written rules about players
having to keep their pants on at all times?' asked George Burns.
The official had to admit the rule book said nothing about this.
'Then leave us alone and go away!' Burns told him. Both men
then proceeded to play the rest of the round in their underwear.

★ ★ ★

Sportscaster Al McGuire was once asked how basketball could be made more exciting. This puzzled him, as he considered that basketball was already the most exciting sport in the world. Finally he replied, 'Eliminate the referees. Raise the basket four feet. Double the size of the basketball. Limit the height of the players to 5 feet 9 inches. Bring back the centre jump. Allow taxi drivers into games for free – and allow the players to carry guns.'

★ ★ ★

Just before the 1988 Olympics, someone had a brilliant idea to save time during the long boxing tournaments. What's more, it was so simple. Have two boxing rings in the hall, rather than one. This way, the boxing event could be over in half the time. Of course, it didn't occur to anyone that the bell ending a round in one ring would be heard in the other. As you would expect, the first time this was tried out, confusion reigned. Some rounds lasted for six minutes. KO punches were landed after the bell. Boxers retired to their corners in the middle of a round, only to be dragged back into the ring by their opponents.

Needless to say, the experiment was judged by the Olympic Committee as a 'failure'.

★ ★ ★

Mark Twain was an enthusiastic angler – and had no respect for official 'seasons'. After spending three weeks in the wilds of New England indulging his passion, he caught a train back to New York. As the journey progressed, he struck up a conversation with an elderly man sitting next to him who asked if he'd been out in the woods.

'I sure have!' said Twain excitedly. 'And let me tell you something. It may be closed season up here in Maine for fishing, but I have 100 pounds of the finest bass you ever saw iced down in the baggage car and headed for home with me!'

Twain asked the old man who he was and what he'd been up to, to which the old man replied, 'I'm a Maine game warden. Who are you?'

'Warden,' Twain replied, 'I'm the biggest liar in the entire United States…'

Football hooligans? Well, there are 92 club chairmen for a start…
– Brian Clough

✱   ✱   ✱

Thomas White of Reigate was not the most skilled of cricketers. Fed up with being constantly bowled out, he turned up for a game between the Chertsey Club against Hambledon on 23 September 1771 with a cricket bat which was far, far wider than the wicket he was defending. He stood there with an incredible look of triumph and his opponents were thoroughly stumped!

That same year, a Mr Garlic, the aptly named captain of the Gardeners, a local Surrey team, used a bat a foot wide, decorated with paintings of vegetables and garden implements. In case you think this was not very sporting, he did have a hole in the middle of it, designed 'to give bowlers a chance'.

This led – rather quickly – to a rule that cricket bats could be no more than $4\frac{1}{2}$ inches wide. (Nowadays the width is $4\frac{1}{4}$ inches.)

✦ ✦ ✦

When it comes to injury time, football referees can't win. In the eyes of fans they either add too much – or too little. Ref Clive Thomas has become equally famous for both extremes. In the 1978 World Cup he ended the match between Brazil and Sweden when the ball was in mid-flight from a corner (the move actually ended in a goal by the Brazilians) while at the opposite end of the spectrum he added 45 minutes of stoppage time to a match that took place on a sloping pitch in Blaengwynfi, Wales. The reason? Every time the ball went out of play it rolled away down a steep hillside and took a while to be recovered.

✦ ✦ ✦

At the time of the 1932 Los Angeles Olympic Games, America was officially a 'dry' country in the grip of Prohibition. The French Olympic team received special permission to import several thousand bottles of wine for their athletes because, they claimed, wine was an essential part of the French diet.

✦ ✦ ✦

Paul Brown, coach of the Cleveland Browns American football team, had the idea of using technology to help his team win – but his idea backfired. For the team's match against the New York Giants in October 1956 he installed a small radio receiver in his quarterback's helmet so he could relay game plays. Brown made the mistake of bragging about his capabilities so

Did you know?
Left-handed polo players are banned by the United States Polo Association.

all the Giants had to do was tune in to his frequency, and eavesdrop. By the time the coach had worked out what was happening the damage had been done. The game finished 21–9 to the Giants.

★   ★   ★

Have you ever wondered why midgets don't play baseball? It's all down to Bill Veeck, owner of the St Louis Browns baseball team. Bill thought it was OK to bend the rules of the game in an effort to win a match against the Detroit Tigers in 1951. The rule that interested him stated that balls must be pitched in a zone between the batter's armpits and his knees. This usually means a space of about $2\frac{1}{2}$ feet. To cause opposing pitchers problems, Bill drafted a midget, Eddie Gaedel, on to his team in 1951, and got him to adopt a crouched stance. This reduced the target area to about two inches. After four mis-pitches, the batsman is allowed to move to first base – which the midget did.

Two days after this controversial tactic, the baseball commissioner's office banned all midgets forever from playing baseball. What's more, the American Baseball League made Gaedel's contract void, claiming it was not in the best interests of baseball. In retaliation, Veeck launched a campaign to stop the authorities discriminating against little people.

★   ★   ★

Committed golfers pride themselves on playing on regardless and members of the Richmond Golf Club in Surrey weren't going to let something like the Battle of Britain interrupt

> Golf is a game in which you yell "fore", shoot six and write down five.
> – American newscaster Paul Harvey

their game in the summer of 1940. Despite the sounds of machine-gun fire, explosions and Spitfires chasing Messerschmitts in the blue skies above, games continued, albeit with a few temporary rules introduced by the Club secretary. These included 'A player whose stroke is affected by the simultaneous explosion of a bomb or shell, or by machine-gun fire, may play another ball from the same place, penalty one stroke' and 'Shrapnel and/or bomb splinters on the fairways, or in bunkers within a club's length of the ball, may be moved without penalty'.

> **Did you know?**
>
> The quickest ever international goal was scored in just eight seconds. Actually, it was scored against England by San Marino, a team of part-timers, in a World Cup qualifier in 1993.

To ensure the safety of its players, the club marked the positions of known delayed-action or unexploded bombs by red flags.

★ ★ ★

Officials at the 1991 Brussels marathon were baffled when the Algerian runner Abbes Tehami came in well ahead of the rest of the field. He looked nothing like the Algerian runner Abbes Tehami who had started the race! For one thing, the Tehami who had just won the race was several inches taller. He was also clean shaven, whereas the Abbes Tehami who had started the race had a thick black moustache. Unless the athlete had grown along the way – and stopped for a shave – something was not quite right. The announcement of a winner for the £4,500 first prize was suspended while officials quickly made enquiries – and discovered that it was Abbes Tehami's coach who had set off from the starting line, run ten miles and then swapped running vests with the real Abbes Tehami who was waiting for him behind a tree. Needless to say, both runners were disqualified.

* * *

Ball tampering isn't just restricted to cricket. Baseball has also been plagued with rumours and allegations. The Dodgers' star pitcher Don Sutton was suspended in 1978 when the umpire found 'foreign substances' on the ball. Whether saliva and/or hair oil, they couldn't find the substances hidden on Sutton himself. When the umpire looked in Sutton's discarded glove all he found was a note that said, 'You're getting warm but it's not in here!'

Pitcher Gaylord Perry was legendary for tampering with the ball to alter its flight. One of his favourite methods was to apply from various parts of his body a combination of spit, sweat, and grease.

* * *

Water and bunkers are the sort of hazards most golfers regularly face, unless, that is, they play in some of the more remote parts of the world. On many public courses in Darwin, North Australia, for example, it's quite common for games to be interrupted by monitor lizards, crocodiles, wallabies and even snakes. Hawks too have become brave enough to swoop down, sink their talons into a ball and carry it off, never to be seen again.

> I don't know. I've never smoked Astroturf.
> – Joe Namath of the New York Jets on being asked whether he preferred Astroturf to grass

In 1961, a game at the Ocean Shores Golf Course near Aberdeen, Washington State was interrupted by a black bear on the fourth fairway. After the players had run for cover the inquisitive creature was driven off by a hastily scrambled helicopter. Revised summer rules for the club were drafted that stated: 'If a ball is picked up by a bear, players may replace and take one penalty stroke. If a player manages to get his ball back from the bear, he may take an automatic par for hole.'

Similar new rules were also introduced at the Elephant Hills Golf Course near the Victoria Falls in Zimbabwe. Terrorist activity around the November 1976 Classic Golf Tournament resulted in this clause: 'A stroke is to be played again if interrupted by gunfire or a sudden explosion.'

The Duke of Windsor once took advantage of the local rules of the Jinja Golf Club in Uganda. These permit the ball to be replaced without penalty if it lands in a hippopotamus footprint.

★　★　★

Since 1974 it's been a criminal offence to cheat at golf anywhere in the state of Ohio. A repeat offender can expect to find himself jailed for up to five years!

★　★　★

Managers and coaches often tell their players to refrain from sex before a game, but one North Korean football manager went a bit too far. In 1964 he made his players stay celibate for the two years leading up to the 1966 World Cup. Whatever you think of that drastic measure, it worked. The team caused one of the major upsets by beating the mighty (but amorous) Italians 1–0 in the final stages of the competition.

Did you know?

Substitutes were only introduced into league football in 1965, and then only for injured players.

Ten years later, just before the 1974 World Cup, the Brazilian manager forced his team to undergo a period of celibacy at their training camp. They were kept away from women for a month, a situation that led one of the players to comment to the press, 'This is supposed to make us world champions. Of what? Masturbation?'

★ ★ ★

Participants at the World Peashooting Championships, held annually at Witcham near Ely, were outraged when one competitor suddenly produced his peashooter, complete with £250 laser-optic gunsight! Unfortunately for him, the gunsight, usually used by hitmen, made the peashooter heavy and wobbly. He lost the contest.

★ ★ ★

'The googly is not unfair – only immoral,' said bowler JHT Bosanquet, the man who invented the action. He adapted it to cricket from the Oxford student game of 'twisti-twosti' in which players try to spin a ball across a table and past their opponent. The first-ever googly was bowled by Bosanquet at Lord's in 1900 in a match between Leicestershire and Middlesex. It is still sometimes called a 'Bosie' by the Australians, who had good cause to remember Bosanquet's Test appearances.

✶   ✶   ✶

During the 1980 Moscow Olympics, Finnish athletes competing in the javelin event accused their Russian rivals of cheating because of 'improper use of the stadium'. They claimed that, when it was a Russian's turn to throw, groundsmen would open the giant stadium doors to let a powerful draught in and 'wind assist' the javelin. Whenever a competitor from any other country came up to compete, the groundsmen would just as quickly pull the doors tight shut again.

✶   ✶   ✶

Today, WG (William Gilbert) Grace enjoys the reputation of being not only a great player but a great sportsman, the English cricketer personified. In reality it was quite different. When bowling, one of his favourite tricks was to point out a non-existent flock of birds in the sky to the opposing batsman, knowing full well that the sun would temporarily blind him.

On one occasion he was bowled out but blamed excess wind for affecting the flight of the ball and refused to leave the crease. In the ensuing argument he reminded the bowler that 'the crowd have come to see me bat, not you bowl!' With that he calmly replaced the bails and carried on.

In another match he hit the ball for what seemed a certain six, only to see a fielder at the boundary positioning himself to make a catch. As the ball dropped down he declared the innings, forcing the umpire to declare him 'not out', since technically the ball had been caught after play had finished.

> When you win the toss, bat. If you are in doubt about it, think – then bat. If you have very big doubts, consult a colleague – then bat.
> – WG Grace

★ ★ ★

Boxer Harry Greb ('The Human Windmill') was blinded in one eye during a fight in 1921 but he managed to keep it a secret from his trainer and all his opponents. Up against Johnny Wilson for the world middleweight title in 1923, he tried to even things up in the sixth round by thumbing his opponent in the eye. The referee pulled both boxers apart and asked Greb what the hell he thought he was doing. Lost for an excuse, Greb snapped back, 'Sticking my thumb in his eye. What does it look like?'

The rest of the fight was played to the rules with Greb winning the world championship on points, the first (and probably only) one-eyed boxer to do so.

CHAPTER 6

Oddballs

'Sports do not build character. They reveal it.'
– sportswriter Heywood Hale Brown

Barry Bremen, an insurance salesman from Detroit, lived out his fantasies of playing professional sports by impersonating players. Before being thrown out he once infiltrated the New York Yankees dug-out, dressed in a home-made uniform. He also played a practice round in the 1980 US Open where he had his photograph taken with Jack Nicklaus, and also pretended he was the ref at an all-star hockey game. His greatest coup, however, was dressing up in drag and appearing with the Dallas Cowboy cheerleaders – before being handcuffed and arrested for trespassing.

★ ★ ★

Lefty Stackhouse was a professional golfer in the 1930s. Although he was a good player he was 'emotional' and liable to fits of extreme tantrums. In one match he was really off form, managing to miss five short putts, carding 81 for the round. He was so mad he decided to vent his anger on his car, a new Model T Ford he'd just bought. Lefty loved his car. It was the one thing he could rely on – unlike his golf. But new or not, Lefty got hold of a club and smashed the windscreen, the radiator and the lights. Next he ripped off a door, slashed the seats, scratched all the body work and even started to dismantle the engine. He told astonished onlookers at the club, 'I felt better after that. It was unavoidable really since my car was the first thing I saw big enough to handle my anger!'

* * *

Dr Renee Richards is unique. She has competed in the US Open Tennis Championships as both a woman and a man (as Richard Ruskine).

* * *

Walking from London to Cambridge and back is quite a feat – but Walter Cornelius did it on his hands. He covered the 153 miles between 2 and 9 April 1968.

✦ ✦ ✦

Jamie Kahakura played for the New Zealand rugby team Weikiki but always seemed strangely reluctant to share the communal bath after a game. His teammates teased him about his prudishness but all was revealed after the Gisborne East Coast competition in 1989. That's when they discovered that Jamie was a woman…

✦ ✦ ✦

As troops from neighbouring Tanzania, led by Julius Nyerere, invaded his country, Ugandan President Idi Amin proposed a novel way to settle the two leaders' differences – a boxing match to be refereed by Muhammad Ali.

Idi Amin had actually been a heavyweight boxer and his proposed fight with the Tanzanian leader signalled a change of tactics. In a previous dispute he'd tried to lull Nyerere into a false sense of security by sending him a telegram that read, 'I love you so much that if you were a woman I would consider marrying you.'

You won't be surprised to hear that the boxing match never took place.

✦ ✦ ✦

Ball boys in soccer were invented because of Chelsea's first goalie. Standing over 6 foot 3 inches and weighing in at 26 stones, Billy Foulke soon earned the rare nickname (for a goalkeeper) of 'Fatty'. Once, he turned down the opportunity of an early-morning

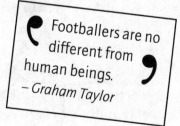

‘ Footballers are no different from human beings.
– Graham Taylor ’

training run and was left on his own at the club. When the other players eventually returned, they found Foulke curled up fast asleep under the dining room table – having just finished eating all eleven breakfasts prepared for the team! On another occasion, he caused a match to be abandoned by swinging on the crossbar and snapping it in two…

A bad-tempered mountain of a man, Foulke used his bulk to intimidate strikers and was known to grab them with one hand and toss them into the back of the netting if they dared to barge him. In 1898 he picked up the Liverpool centre forward George Allan and, holding his boots in one hand, dunked him up and down in the mud like a biscuit in a mug of tea. Not surprisingly, a penalty was awarded against him. Foulke's antics meant he was jeered and heckled by opposing fans. This had no effect whatsoever on the gargantuan goalie who said, 'I don't mind what they call me, as long as they don't call me late for lunch.'

It must be noted that the strikers gave as good as they got in return, often retaliating by aiming their volleys straight at Foulke's most vulnerable point – his large flabby stomach. In one match, striker Steve Bloomer knocked Foulke down with a well-aimed shot to the belly. It cannoned off the keeper and Foulke just had time to pick himself up before Bloomer launched another devastating shot that had him flat on his back yet again. By the time Bloomer regained possession, he had an open goal to aim at. Foulke had fled the goalmouth!

> Nobody I've ever played with has said "Sick as a parrot" when I've asked them how they were. But thrust a microphone in front of them and it all comes out: "It was a game of two halves", "We'll take each match as it comes", "The boy done good". We have caught it from them – we're as sick as a commentator.
> – Gary Lineker

To help Fatty Foulke intimidate strikers, Chelsea employed two small boys to stand behind his goal and yell out things like, 'Isn't he a size?' and 'They'll never get the ball past him!' Soon, they were helping the slow and lumbering keeper to retrieve balls from behind the goal or in the stands – and the tradition of the ballboy was established.

★ ★ ★

Henry Lewis, a champion billiards player in the 1920s, once sank 45 consecutive balls – using his nose as the cue.

★ ★ ★

Eddie Shore of the Boston Bruins ice hockey team in the 1920s had a reputation for being quite a tough guy. He once broke three ribs colliding with the goal posts at a game in New York. His examining doctor tried to arrange a hospital bed for him, but by the time he returned, Eddie had vanished. He'd caught a train to Montreal where, the next day, ignoring his acute pain, he scored two goals for his team.

Another time he was involved in a punch-up with opponents that left him unconscious on the ice for ten minutes. The first words he spoke after coming round having suffered severe cuts to his face, a broken nose, gashed mouth and several broken teeth were, 'This is all part of ice hockey.'

★ ★ ★

George Gunn was a successful county cricketer, scoring 35,000 runs for Nottinghamshire between 1902 and 1932. He did, however, like his food and nothing would stand between him and his lunch, not even a championship cricket match. On one occasion his team were playing Hampshire. Gunn was batting when the pavilion clock reached 1.30 pm. The batsman assumed this was the break for lunch, removed the bails and started to walk off the pitch. He was stopped by the umpire who told him that lunch was being taken at 2 pm that day. Gunn calmly walked back to the wicket and replaced the bails, then stood to face the Hampshire bowler. As the ball was thrown, Gunn stepped neatly to one side, letting the ball clatter against his middle stump. Now out, he once again began his walk to the pavilion, telling his astonished teammates, 'I always take my lunch at 1.30 pm.'

★ ★ ★

> Better make it six, I can't eat eight.
> – Dan Osinski, US baseball player on being asked by a waitress whether he wanted his pizza cut into six or eight pieces

Basketball superstar Dennis Rodman of the Chicago Bulls launched his biography in 1996 – *Bad As I Wanna Be*. Nothing unusual with that, except that he decided to wear a wedding dress at the book launch, claiming that he liked to bring out his feminine side. He promised something even more spectacular for his last game, telling reporters, 'I'll walk off the court and take off one piece of clothing with each step. Then I'll be about mid-court and I'll walk the rest of the way into the locker room nude.'

✱   ✱   ✱

In 1968, American Steve McPeak rode his 13-foot unicycle from Chicago to Los Angeles, taking six weeks to cover the 2,000 miles. Just one question. Why?

✱   ✱   ✱

In 1939 Joe 'Mule' Sprinz, a catcher with the Cleveland Indians baseball team, attempted to get into the record books by making the 'world's highest catch'. In his case it was a baseball dropped from a plane flying at 1,000 feet. He missed the first four balls thrown out but caught the fifth, which glanced off his face into his hands. He gained a place in the *Guinness Book of Records* but lost four teeth in the process. It was estimated that the ball was travelling at 100 mph when it hit him.

✱   ✱   ✱

French racing driver Jean Behra didn't carry a rabbit's foot as a good-luck charm; he carried a spare right ear. His real one had been severed in a crash in 1955 and was replaced with a life-like plastic one. In case it should fall off, or become otherwise detached, Behra always kept the spare ear in a

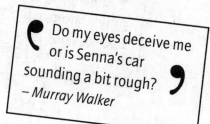

Do my eyes deceive me or is Senna's car sounding a bit rough?
– Murray Walker

container in his pocket. For a joke he would chat up a woman, then astound her by calmly removing his right ear at an opportune moment.

* * *

At 20–1, Sweet Kiss was by no means a dead cert to win a steeplechase at Belmont Park in 1925 – but his jockey was. Rider Frank Hayes passed away from natural causes during the race and was dead when he crossed the finish line, the first deceased jockey to win a race.

* * *

Managers like Arsène Wenger and Alex Ferguson are admired for their cool approach to the game and calm temperament. Sunderland manager Johnny Cochrane was in this league, with a very cavalier attitude towards his team's opposition. While he was in charge between 1928 and 1939 he would pop his head round his team's dressing room door just before a match, and ask who Sunderland were playing. On being told he'd just nod and say, 'That's all right. We'll piss that lot,' before leaving for the sidelines.

> It's a desperately close race – I can't quite tell who is ahead. It's either Oxford or Cambridge…
> – John Snagge, commentating for BBC Radio at the 1952 Boat Race

CHAPTER 7

Money Isn't Everything

'The only man who makes money following the races is the one who does so with a broom and shovel'
– *Elbert Hubbard*

Today's inflated transfer fees can really go to a player's head and make him feel over-important. But the reverse can also be true. Consider how Daniel Allende must have felt after his transfer from second division Uruguayan side Central Español to first division Rentistas in 1979. Despite being a first division side, Rentistas was a little short of cash. However, their president owned a slaughterhouse and so swapped rising star Allende for a grand total of 550 beefsteaks, to be paid in instalments of 25 steaks a week…

Incidentally, in 1937 Gillingham transferred one of its players to Aston Villa for the princely sum of three second-hand turnstiles, two goalkeeper's sweaters, three cans of weedkiller and an old typewriter.

> ❝ I'm going to write a book, *How To Make A Small Fortune In Baseball*. First, you start with a large fortune…
> – *Robert Carpentier III, sports entrepreneur* ❞

✶ ✶ ✶

It's rumoured that some Premier League footballers earn upwards of £40,000 per week but spare a thought for the poor old players of Brazilian club Londrina. Strapped for cash, it had to pay its players' win bonuses in the form of cattle.

Faced with a similar situation in 1961, Istanbul footballer Ridvan Sracoglu withdrew his life savings and presented them to his ailing club.

✶ ✶ ✶

American baseball teams have tried all sorts of strange promotions to encourage more spectators to attend. In 1979 the Chicago White Sox held an anti-disco night, offering admittance to a double-header for 98 cents to anyone who arrived with a disco record. The idea was that the records would be burned after the first game. Unfortunately, records started littering the playing field *during* the first game. When the records were eventually burned, the spectacle so incited the anti-disco feelings of fans that they stormed on to the field tearing up the bases and starting fires. After 37 arrests the field was declared unplayable and the second game abandoned.

❝ Well I had a better year.
— Babe Ruth (when asked to comment whether it was fair that in 1930 he earned more than the President of the United States, Herbert Hoover) ❞

Not as disastrous, but still disappointing, was a promotion held by the Philadelphia 76ers. Their 'Blind Date' night allocated odd-numbered seats to men and even-numbered seats to women. Fifty-six men turned up but only four women.

★ ★ ★

When world heavyweight champ Mike Tyson knocked out challenger Michael Spinks in Atlantic City in 1988 with just eight punches, his income from the fight worked out at $2.5 million per punch.

In 1997 he earned $75 million and became the highest-paid athlete in the entire history of sport. If he hadn't got so peckish during his fight with Evander Holyfield, he would surely have earned even more the following year...

★ ★ ★

Developers are infamous for buying up sports grounds and turning them into supermarkets or offices. A contractor in Fiji had enough clout to get a cricket pitch moved because it was too near to building work. This resulted in fielders finding themselves standing in the sea during games when the tide was in.

★ ★ ★

In the mid-1970s, America was reeling at the salaries top
sportsmen were receiving. When one commentator asked
Philadelphia Phillies star pitcher Tony 'Tug' McGraw how he'd be
spending his then colossal salary of $75,000, 'Tug' replied, '90 per
cent I'll spend on good times, women and Irish whiskey. The
other 10 per cent I'll probably waste…'

★ ★ ★

In June 1995, the stadium belonging to Brazilian side Flamengo
was filled with one of the strangest crowds ever seen at a football
match. The stands were packed full of hundreds upon hundreds
of dogs, assembled as a neat publicity stunt to watch new player
Edmundo, 'The Animal', turn out for his new club for the first
time.

✦ ✦ ✦

In 1957 it was discovered that basketball referee John Fraser was in collusion with a big betting syndicate in America's mid-west, rigging games for cash. When confronted by the authorities he admitted his crimes but was allowed to 'retire' in order to avoid a huge scandal.

When news eventually did leak out it didn't surprise a lot of players. One of them, Little Joe, who played for the University of Wichita, thought something was up because of the way that Fraser would have quiet words with the players, offering them advice as to how to play the game, 'When he'd hand you the ball he'd say something like "Now you're ahead, hang on to the ball. Stall. Stall…".'

✦ ✦ ✦

In 1967 CBS tried to popularise soccer in the US by televising matches – but they soon encountered one problem. Unlike American football which has plenty of time-outs that are ideal for showing commercials, soccer has just one – between the two halves. CBS tried to slip in ads when players were injured, or when the ball went out of play, but these opportunities were far too short. On one famous occasion an injured Toronto player was getting up, when he was pushed back down again by

❝ The Internal Revenue Service is the real undefeated heavyweight champion. They show you the left. You never see the right. They'll take everything, even your tears.
– George Foreman ❞

referee Peter Rhodes – all because the commercial being shown wasn't quite over.

Soon after that CBS abandoned broadcasting soccer.

* * *

> I've got a bad swing, a bad stance and a bad grip, but my banker loves me.
> – Lee Trevino

Golf Digest magazine estimates that the odds of achieving a hole in one are 33,616 – 1. In Japan, you can take out insurance against hitting a hole in one – because, by tradition, you then have to host a party for the golf club members and shower your golfing partners, your caddy and all your friends with expensive gifts – as well as planting a commemorative tree on the course. A hole in one has been known to cost Japanese golfers almost £3,000!

* * *

When tennis players win a tournament they're usually presented with a symbolic empty envelope, with the real cheque following on later. Martina Navratilova discovered that it always pays to make sure. She won the Virginia Slims Tennis Tournament in New York and after being presented with her envelope, threw it away as she got outside the courts. What she didn't know was that it contained the real cheque, for hundreds of thousands of dollars.

Fortunately, a search of the rubbish bin later on turned up the missing prize money.

* * *

The 1993 World Cup qualifier between Spain and Albania was over. It had been a hard-fought game, but the Spanish side had come to respect their opponents and started to swap shirts with them as they left the pitch. To their surprise, the Albanians clung to their kit for dear life, shaking their heads furiously and making off quickly for the showers. The Spanish players were non-plussed. Had they offended the Albanians somehow? Later they learned that the Albanian national team couldn't afford to buy any more. In fact, the game had nearly been forfeited by the little Balkan side because they were three shirts short beforehand. Only a desperate search by the entire team had turned up three spare shirts…

★ ★ ★

After serious irregularities in payments to players, Leeds City Football Club was officially closed down by the FA in 1919. Players and management found themselves assembled at Leed's Hotel Metropole where they were to be auctioned off! The entire team raised about £10,000 in total, with players being bought for as little as £250.

★ ★ ★

Proving that good manners cost nothing, Italian footballer Graziano Landoni was fined £600 in 1971 for not saying goodbye to his trainer when he left the club Palermo. The action was instigated by the Italian players' union.

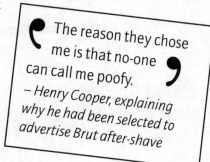

The reason they chose me is that no-one can call me poofy.
– Henry Cooper, explaining why he had been selected to advertise Brut after-shave

* * *

The Football Association investigated an illegal payment to one of the Fulham players after their January 1958 FA Cup tie win against Bristol Rovers. It happened because director Tommy Trinder offered an incentive bonus to the first player to score a hat trick. Arthur Stevens did so and won the bonus – Trinder's overcoat.

CHAPTER 8

The Luck of the Draw

'The hallmark of a great captain is to win the toss
at the right time'
– *Richie Benaud*

Golfer Jim Cash had an amazing hole in one at the Belmont
Springs Country Club in Massachusetts. In November 1929 he
hit his ball to the sixteenth green where it rested gingerly at the
rim of the cup. As he stepped away from the tee, Jim and his
opponent felt a small earth tremor – sufficient enough to drop
the ball in the hole.

If that wasn't bizarre enough, how about the shot played by
Canadian Jack Ackerman at the Bay of Quinte Club in Ontario
back in 1934. Again, his tee shot came to rest on the edge of the
hole – but was helped in by a butterfly which landed on it!

★　★　★

In the nineteenth century, an amateur English sporting
enthusiast took his fiancée out for a day at the races. Not
knowing a lot about form, he asked his girlfriend to choose the

horse she liked the look of. Naturally, she chose a horse that looked rather splendid, but had never come close to winning a race in its life. Nevertheless, the sportsman backed it with all the money he had that day and, incredibly, it romped home.

With his new-found wealth, the sportsman sailed to California and invested all his money in real estate. It proved to be a shrewd investment and as his holdings increased, he decided to name the area of land he now owned after the obscure horse he'd backed on his fiancée's whim – Hollywood.

★ ★ ★

The prize pike that hangs on the wall in Les King's Norfolk home wasn't caught – it was hit on the head and killed outright by his shot from the 17th hole on his local golf course .

A PIKE IN ONE

★ ★ ★

At the US Open in 1968, Dutch tennis star Tom 'The Flying Dutchman' Okker walked away with the $14,000 first prize, even though he'd lost. Arthur Ashe, his opponent, was an amateur and therefore couldn't receive any prize money.

* * *

In a strange quirk of fate, Denmark only qualified for the European Championships in 1992 because Yugoslavia had suddenly erupted in a bloody civil war and had dropped out of the tournament. The Danes went on to lift the trophy, beating Germany 2–0 in the final.

* * *

A hole in one is a truly spectacular – and statistically very unlikely – feat. If you witness one, you can consider yourself pretty fortunate. So imagine how the assembled crowds at the Oak Hill Country Club in Rochester, New York felt when they witnessed not one – but a staggering four holes in one on the same hole in the same round.

It was the 1989 US Open Golf Championship. First, Doug Weaver aced the 159-yard sixth hole with his seven-iron shot. An hour and ten minutes later, Mark Wiebe scored his hole in one there. Then Jerry Pate, then Nick Price. It was the first time in golfing history that such an unlikely event had been recorded. How unlikely? Since 1938, when records began, there had only been 17 holes in one recorded in the US Open. The event so intrigued Harvard professor of mathematics Joseph Harris that he decided to do a few calculations on the likelihood of four holes in one in the same hole during the same tournament. He decided the odds against it happening were 1.89 quadrillion to one! According to John P. Everhart, president of the National Hole in One Foundation, such an extraordinary tournament, statistically speaking, won't happen again now for another 190 years.

> In the United States I'm lucky. In Europe I'm good.
> – Seve Ballesteros

* * *

The American ski jumper Chuck Ryan was competing in an event in Duluth, Minnesota in 1959. As Chuck left the ramp, both his skis became detached from his boots. To the amazement of the spectators he travelled on for 150 feet, managing to get his legs out in front of him to cushion the impending impact. He touched down, skidded another 100 feet before coming to a safe halt in the soft snow. Here he calmly dusted himself off and walked away. According to Ryan, his trick was 'to come sliding in like a ball player into second'.

* * *

Manchester City goalie Bert Trautmann knew he had hurt himself after diving for the ball at the feet of Birmingham's Peter Murphy during the 1956 FA Cup Final, but he had no idea just how badly. He carried on playing and helped to see his team to a 3–1 victory, before picking up his winner's medal and heading off to hospital. The doctors who examined him couldn't believe he was still alive. He had played the last fifteen minutes of the match with a broken neck.

* * *

> I fought Sugar Ray Robinson so many times it's a wonder I don't have diabetes.
> – Jake LaMotta

In 1912, Jack Johnson, the world's first black heavyweight boxing champion, was refused permission to board an ocean liner sailing from Britain to New York because of his colour. The *Titanic* sailed without him.

★   ★   ★

In 1961 Louisa Murray was struck on the head by a bowling ball dropped from a great height – and lived to tell the tale. As a result, she ended up appearing in an advertising campaign… for watches. How? Well it all began when Louisa was innocently sitting at an outdoor café in Burlington, Vermont. Above the restaurant was an apartment block where one of the third-floor occupants had been cleaning his bowling ball on the kitchen table. Unfortunately the ball did what it was designed to do – roll. It rolled off the table and through the open window, glancing off Louisa's head and then her wrist.

Unbelievably, Louisa only suffered concussion although she did break one thing – the glass of her Timex watch. The watch itself, however, continued to run. Someone from Timex read about Louisa's lucky escape in the paper and contacted her to see if they could use her story to promote their watches. She agreed and, thanks to that bowling ball, Louisa became a star promoting Timex, the watch that 'takes a lickin' and keeps on tickin''.

★   ★   ★

It was the most terrifying ride of National Hunt jockey Fred Winter's life. Even before the 1962 Grand Steeplechase de Paris started, Winter was so ill that he needed help to get dressed in his colours and onto his mount, Mandarin. Then, just three fences into the race, the bit snapped between Mandarin's teeth, which meant that Winter had next to no control over his horse. For three miles he clung on for dear life, steering as best he could with his knees and heels and pulling frantically

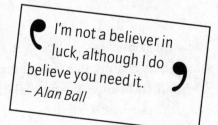

I'm not a believer in luck, although I do believe you need it.
– Alan Ball

on the horse's neck. All he cared about was staying on and, once past the finish line, couldn't believe it when he was told he'd actually won the race.

Winter later said that victory was all down to Mandarin. 'What could I do?' he said. 'I couldn't steer him, I couldn't stop and I was too frightened to jump off!'

★　★　★

Peter Croke was playing golf at the Southerndown Golf Club near Porthcawl in Wales when he got a hole in one with a difference. He hit a wild shot on the seventeenth fairway and his ball got lodged in a sheep's backside. The sheep, who had been grazing peacefully, was so startled that it ran off towards the green – with the ball still firmly stuck. It did eventually get shaken loose but by then it was thirty yards nearer the *right* hole, making it a much easier shot for Peter.

★　★　★

Many sportsmen have quirky little superstitions before a game which, they claim, can make all the difference to the outcome.

Southend United player Phil Gridelet always insisted on being the last Southend player to come on to the pitch at the beginning of each half. This was usually straightforward enough – until the day when his team played Ipswich in February 1997. A teammate was having problems with his contact lenses and so missed the start of the second half.

> I don't think we'll go down. But then again, the captain of the *Titanic* said the same thing.
> – Neville Southhall, talking about Everton's chances of staying in the Premier League

This meant that Gridelet had to remain with him as well – to ensure he was the last Southend player on to the pitch. This ridiculous situation meant that Southend started the second half not one, but two men short, a situation described by their manager Ronnie Whelan, rather generously, as 'crazy'.

Other superstitious footballers have included Roberto Rivelino, the Brazilian midfield genius, who believed that his team would be successful as long as he kept his moustache. His colleague Pele always wore the number ten shirt and would only stay in hotel rooms with the same number. David Fairclough of Liverpool was said to wash his hands four times before a game. It was even reported that former Birmingham City manager Ron Saunders asked players to paint the soles of their shoes red in order to avoid an ancient gypsy curse.

★ ★ ★

Tennis champion Bjorn Borg had a whole series of superstitious rituals. He would stop shaving four days before a championship. He would arrange his racquets in descending order of tension, testing each one meticulously for up to an hour. He also insisted that the cars that took him to Wimbledon always had to have a stereo radio fitted – even if it wasn't used. He would always travel to Wimbledon over Hammersmith Bridge – never Putney Bridge.

His mother Margarethe was as bad as her son. For luck she always made sure she was sucking a boiled sweet when watching the final set. In the 1979 Wimbledon final, Borg failed to convert three match points against Roscoe Tanner and Margarethe spat the sweet on to the floor, the first time she'd done so. She immediately picked it up and put it back in her mouth. Borg then won.

★　★　★

Formula One drivers are also a superstitious bunch. Alex Wurz, the Benetton driver, used to go racing wearing a red boot on his left foot and a blue one on his right foot. He had won a race early on in his career wearing odd boots after a teammate had hidden one of them as a practical joke.

David Coulthard only ever gets into his McLaren right foot first, from the left-hand side, but he has the added superstition of making sure he wears his lucky pants for each race. This is a long-running tradition except that the pants have become so old and hole-ridden that they can't be worn in the 'normal' fashion any more – he now has to wear them over his fireproofs, much like Superman.

★　★　★

Professional golfers are also not immune to superstition. Gary Player only plays with even-numbered balls while Seve Ballesteros won't touch a number-three ball. Tom Weiskopf, however, likes the number three and always carries three coins in his pocket when he plays.

Lee Trevino doesn't like the number thirteen – but with good reason. He was playing in the 1975 Western Open when he was hit by lightning at the thirteenth hole. The match took place on the thirteenth day of the month and Bobby Nichols and Jerry Heard were also struck. All three survived but they all had to be hospitalised.

★ ★ ★

As for boxers, Ken Norton was absolutely terrified of black cats. To ensure good luck Henry Cooper never polished his boots, Joe Louis always insisted on putting his left glove on before his right while the world light-heavyweight champion of the mid-1960s, Willy Pastrano, tied his wedding ring to his left bootlace. Muhammad Ali always wore his 'lucky' robe. I'm not sure about the 'luck' aspect but it was definitely special – it was given to him by Elvis Presley.

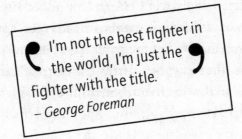

I'm not the best fighter in the world, I'm just the fighter with the title.
– George Foreman

CHAPTER 9

It's a Funny Old Game

'Baseball is 90 per cent mental. The other half is physical'
– Yogi Berra, New York Yankees baseball player

Lots of football matches can be described as walkovers, but one that actually was took place in Chile in November 1973. The national team were drawn against the Russians for a place in the 1974 World Cup Finals. The first match, played in Moscow, was a 0–0 draw. Before the away leg, General Pinochet staged a coup in Chile, which led to the deaths of thousands of dissidents. The Russians then tried to make a political point by refusing to send a team to Chile but FIFA wouldn't have any of it. The match duly went ahead – without the Russians. Of course, with no opposition the Chileans scored in seconds and went through to the World Cup Finals in Germany.

★　★　★

If you fancy having a flutter on armadillo racing (and let's face it, who doesn't) visit Fort Worth in Texas. The sport's big there with the creatures' human owners chasing them along the course, shouting words of encouragement.

Visit Angels Camp in California and you can watch jumping frogs compete with each other. The two-day event is known as Calaveras County Jumping Frog Jubilee and attracts 40,000 entrants from as far afield as South America, England and even Australia. The all-time record was held for years by a swamp frog called Corrision who jumped 18 feet and half an inch in May 1970. However, in May 1980 this was shattered by a Salinas frog called Oh-No, who leapt into the record books with an amazing 19 feet, 9½ inches.

The rules are simple. Each frog makes three consecutive jumps, in as straight a line as possible – with the total distance counting.

★ ★ ★

As its name suggests, the 'Titanic Award' is won by the most magnificent boat to sink in the Great Cardboard Boat Regatta, held annually in Sheboygan, Wisconsin. Vessels entered must be built from corrugated cardboard and have to navigate a 200-yard course four times. The boats can be crewed by up to two people and can be any shape or size – providing that only cardboard is used in their construction.

★   ★   ★

Lady golfers playing at the Kingarth Links on the Isle of Bute in
the summer of 1970 scattered in all directions when a torpedo
streaked out of the water and came to rest on the first green.
Representatives from the Royal Navy turned up later to rather
sheepishly ask if they could have their torpedo back.

★   ★   ★

On 12 December 1891, Blackburn Rovers and Burnley played
one of the strangest games in the record books. The temperature
had dropped below zero and driving sleet was whipping across
the pitch, but it did nothing to cool an increasingly hot-tempered
game. Two players got into a fist fight and the referee sent them
both off. The remaining Blackburn outfield players rushed over
to complain about the decision and were so aggressive that the
referee sent them all off too. Now only Blackburn goalie Herbie
Arthur was left to face the ten men of Burnley. Deprived of any
defenders, he could hardly be blamed when Burnley scored after
just a few minutes. While the Burnley strikers were still
celebrating, Arthur appealed to the referee that the goal was
technically offside as there were no Blackburn players except the
goalie on the field. Exasperated, freezing cold and thoroughly
perplexed, the referee decided first to award
Blackburn a free kick –
and then changed his
mind and decided to
abandon the match
entirely!

> The spirit at this club is
> the worst I've ever known,
> and the tea's not
> much better either.
> – Dave Bassett
> (on Sheffield United)

★ ★ ★

I'm glad I didn't have to commentate at any of the matches
played by the Danish national soccer team in the 1950s. There
were sometimes six players in the side all called Nielsen. It's a
commentator's worst nightmare. 'The ball's with Nielsen. Passes
to Nielsen. Back to Nielsen. Over to Nielsen. He's got Nielsen and
Nielsen up there with him in support…' You see what I mean.
For the record, the offending players were Rick Moller Nielsen,
Verner Nielsen, Erling Nielsen, Hans C Nielsen, Ove Bech Nielsen
and Flemming Nielsen.

★ ★ ★

Golfers have to be careful playing at Laurens Golf and Country
Club in Iowa. The main hazard here isn't low-flying balls but
low-flying planes. You see, the course doubles as an airport with
the single grass 1,200-foot runway cutting through the rough and
fairways of seven holes.

Golfers have to be patient, contending with crop dusters and
small single-engined planes that touch down every now and
then. Of course, the aircraft have right of way but some golfers
don't take kindly to their game being interrupted. Some have
been know to smash runway lights with their clubs. Other just
stand where they are and take their shots, causing planes to abort
their approach. Others do
move away, but in a show of
solidarity, conveniently
'forget' to take their golf
carts with them, leaving
them on the runway.

A golfer teeing off at a
course in Livermore,

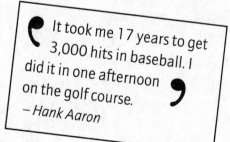

It took me 17 years to get
3,000 hits in baseball. I
did it in one afternoon
on the golf course.
– Hank Aaron

California, once hit the ball just a little too enthusiastically. It smashed through the side window of an aircraft coming in to land at an airport near the course and hit the pilot on the head. Luckily, he was still able to land the plane.

In the 1820s, chess players all along the eastern seaboard of the United States were thrashed by a mechanical chess player. The device was toured around the country by its Austrian inventor Johann Maelzel. Nicknamed 'The Turk', the device consisted of an expressionless wooden man seated behind a chess board on a solid wooden desk. Players sat facing 'The Turk', who was cranked up, ready for action.

Each human move was met with a mechanical whirring and clicking as the Turk's wooden arms jerked to a playing piece, picked it up and moved it. The robot chess player could usually checkmate an opponent within an hour.

The machine was the talk of America until 1837, when a bitter former associate of the Austrian inventor spilled the beans. The Turk was actually controlled by a chess-playing midget, who hid inside the mechanism. With the secret out, everyone lost interest. Maelzel went broke, hit the bottle and died within a year, a broken man.

What sport do you get if you cross the Japanese love for Sumo wrestling with their skill in electronic miniaturisation? That's right, 'Robot Sumo'. In the event, first held in 1989, radio-controlled robots knock each other out of a ring to win their owners a first prize of one million yen.

One sport where spitting isn't anti-social, it's a necessity, is the annual National Tobacco-Spitting Contest held in Raleigh, Mississippi. The record is held by Don Snyder (31 feet 1 inch) who practised for the finals by spitting for two hours every day for a month. One of the greats in the Tobacco Spitting Hall of Fame is George Craft, known as the Babe Ruth of tobacco spitters. He retired aged 75 after holding 14 consecutive long-distance records. He claimed he inherited his spitting prowess from his mother. According to George, 'She could hit the fireplace from any spot in the room – and never even got a dab on the floor.'

But this year, over in Edgerton, Wisconsin, anti-smoking protesters had their way by getting the annual tobacco-spitting contest banned. In its place was the much less controversial watermelon seed-spitting contest. This failed to find favour with the locals, as not one contestant turned up to enter.

★   ★   ★

If you like chariot racing, and you love chickens, then get along to Wynard, a small town in Saskatchewan, Canada. There, small hand-built chariots are harnessed to chickens who then race down a 50-foot track.

* * *

It's a glamorous life in the world of professional tiddlywinks. In 1961, Britain's top tiddlywinks team 'The Twinkies' went on a tour of Africa, defeating some of the continent's crack teams. The pinnacle of their success, both figuratively and literally, was when they thrashed a 'Commonwealth All Stars' tiddlywinks team in a match played on top of Mount Kilimanjaro.

* * *

Animal lovers shouldn't play football in Turkey. Before certain matches a sheep is sacrificed in the middle of the pitch and the fresh, warm blood is then smeared over players' faces as a good-luck charm. If you think that's uncivilised then don't go to Nairobi as a goalkeeper. To bring them luck, some footballers urinate on the ball just before kick-off.

* * *

As part of a rehabilitation scheme, authorities in Salta, Argentina, sanctioned a football match between prisoners and a local team. The match started well but soon degenerated into mayhem when all 22 players ended up fighting. The fracas started when two of the prisoners recognised one of their opponents as the police officer who'd put them inside.

★　　★　　★

One of the most unusual racing clubs in the world must be the All-Alaskan Racing Pigs Club. With a motto of 'Come rain or swine, the sow must go on', they host the annual All-Alaskan Racing Pigs Finals, where eight championship porkers compete to be the fastest thing on four trotters.

★　　★　　★

Workers at the Jet Propulsion Laboratory in Pasadena, California play unicycle hockey. As its name suggests, players ride on unicycles, using elongated hockey sticks to flick the puck up and down a court.

If you don't have a good sense of balance but you do possess a great pair of lungs you might want to try the increasingly popular sport of underwater hockey. There are yearly play-offs to determine the best US team and they also hold a world championship. The event was dreamed up in 1954 by British scuba divers who needed an activity to keep them fit in the winter. The game is played at the bottom of a swimming pool where two teams of six try to push a brass puck into their opponent's goal.

> Billiards is very similar to snooker, except there are only three balls and no one watches it.
> – Steve Davis

★ ★ ★

It has yet to make it on to our TV screens in England, but the big sporting craze now sweeping Sweden is rabbit show-jumping. It's just like the Horse of the Year show, except with rabbits, who jump miniature fences against the clock. There's even a water jump.

★ ★ ★

The American equivalent of the RSPCA successfully campaigned for the banning of a unique form of sport during a Florida music festival – pig skydiving. Similarly, pressure was put on the organisers of a rodeo in California to cancel a tournament where steers were wrestled to the ground by teams of three men. As if this wasn't bad enough, the contest was only over when the teams had managed to put women's underwear on the animals.

★   ★   ★

Conscription made life difficult for many football clubs during the Second World War. Many couldn't scrape together eleven men to field a team and so had to borrow players from other clubs or invite members of the crowd to climb out of the stands and hurriedly don a kit. On Christmas Day 1940, Brighton set off for Norwich with only five players. They made up their team with some Norwich reserves and a few soldiers from the crowd, but were still beaten 18–0! On the same day, Tommy Lawton played twice – once for Everton against Liverpool in the morning and then again for Tranmere against Crewe, where he scored both Tranmere's goals.

The great English soccer player Stan Mortensen played his first international match *against* England. In September 1943, he was an England reserve. The Welsh national team 'borrowed' him to replace one of their injured players and Mortensen took to the pitch in Welsh colours. His side lost 8–3. Mortensen wouldn't get to play for his own country until 1947 when 'the Electric Eel'– as he became known – scored four goals in England's 10–0 trouncing of Portugal in Lisbon.

★   ★   ★

Snow, bad light or fog have been known to stop a football match, but what about lightning? It happened during the replay of the Army Cup Final football match between the Royal Artillery and the Royal Armoured Corps at a pitch in Aldershot in April 1948. The first match ended 0–0 but

Did you know?
Both Derby County and Aston Villa didn't start out as football clubs. They were both originally set up to play baseball.

99

the replay was far more eventful. During the second half it began to rain, and thunder could be heard in the distance. The referee blew for a free kick but just as he was taking the whistle from his lips, it was hit by a bolt of lightning. The ref and eight nearby players were thrown to the ground. Tragically two died and the rest were treated for burns. Astonishingly, despite taking the full force of the lightning bolt, the referee escaped unscathed.

A similar occurrence happened at a match in Mexico in 1964. Four players plus the referee were hit by lightning and taken to hospital. They were OK – or would have been if the ambulance hadn't crashed into a bus on the way there!

★ ★ ★

Everyone's heard of dwarf tossing but does it really take place? The answer is yes, it does – at least in Australia. It was invented at a Queensland bar in 1985 where someone had the bright idea of strapping padding and a crash helmet to a dwarf, and hurling

him across the bar room into a pile of mattresses – the furthest throw deciding the winner. Some dwarfs have been thrown 30 feet. Why do they do it? Well, it's hard to turn down the chance to make as much as £1,000 per night.

✶ ✶ ✶

Fed up secretaries should move to Manchester in New Hampshire. There they can take part in an annual typewriter tossing competition.

✶ ✶ ✶

It wasn't rain or bad light that stopped play on the first day of the India–Pakistan Test in 1979 – it was a swarm of bees. Players and officials were forced to lie flat on the ground and cover their ears with their hands for several minutes as the swarm hovered over them.

✶ ✶ ✶

Portisham in Devon has a place in sporting history. It's the first – and last – place in the world to play host to cat racing. In 1936, sporting entrepreneurs built the world's first cat racetrack there, complete with electric mice. The public certainly liked the idea and flocked to the early races, but the cats weren't interested at all. When the traps came open, most preferred to stay curled up asleep inside. Those who did come out racing usually preferred fighting each other to chasing the mouse, and the stadium was soon closed down…

> Poland nil, England nil, though England are now looking better value for their nil.
> – Barry Davies

★ ★ ★

English fans might smile at the unusual names of some Scottish football clubs but Partick Thistle, Queen of the South or Hamilton Academical fade into insignificance when you consider some foreign team names: How about the Venomous Vipers, Hearts of Oak and the Mysterious Dwarfs (from Ghana), Zurich Grasshoppers, the Young Boys of Bern and the Young Fellow Zurich (Switzerland), Boom (Belgium), Los Terribles (Peru), Stationery Stores FC and Julius Berger (Nigeria), Kickers Offenbach (Germany), The Invincible Eleven (Liberia), Nimbles Rail, Always Ready and The Strongest (Bolivia) and Red Boys Differ (Luxembourg). As strange as they may seem, they can't compare with the Finnish third division team FC Santa Claus, Colon from Argentina or the brilliant Panto Rosso Sexy Shop (Italy).

★ ★ ★

In 1937, Romford Greyhound Stadium decided to stage a world first in sporting events. The public seemed to be getting a little jaded about conventional greyhound racing and attendances were falling. As a solution, the owners decided to try cheetah racing. After all, what could be more exciting than seeing the world's fastest land animals racing each other at speeds of over 70 miles an hour! Unfortunately, on the day of the big race, things didn't work out as planned. You see, if several cheetah are all chasing the same prey, as soon as one pulls out in the lead the others all say 'Fine, it's yours mate' and sit down and have a rest. And that's exactly what happened.

Did you know?
Spanish soccer team Real Valladolid once had a striker called Marlon Brando.

In desperation, the owners then tried to raise bets on the speed of a single cheetah chasing the rabbit on its own. However, the solitary cheetah very quickly worked out that all he had to do was lie down on the track and let the rabbit come back round to him…

Cheetah racing, needless to say, has not been tried again since.

★ ★ ★

The honour of being the first and only US President to have invented a new sport went to Herbert Hoover. In 1929, in an effort to help him keep in shape, Hoover and five of his aides played a game that consisted of throwing a nine-pound medicine ball over a volleyball net. The game was scored like tennis and became known as 'Hooverball'. A spokesman for the President described the game as 'sort of like throwing a frozen turkey back and forth over a garage roof'. Today an annual Hooverball tournament is held at West Branch, Iowa, Hoover's birthplace.

★ ★ ★

Trying to transport the Olympic torch from Greece to the host nation is fraught with difficulties. In 1976 the torch went out in the rain en route to the 1976 Montreal Olympics, and an official had to re-light it with a rolled-up newspaper and a lighter.

Eight years earlier, on the way to Mexico City, the torch carrier was intercepted by Corsican bandits in Grenoble, France, who tried to steal it and hold it to ransom. They

> Pro wrestling is amateur wrestling with everything boring taken out of it.
> – Brian Glover, actor and ex-wrestler

gave up when they discovered there were four back-up torches, held just in case of such an eventuality.

★   ★   ★

The most confused football match in history took place at White Hart Lane in 1945. Arsenal had borrowed the pitch from Spurs to play a friendly match against Dynamo Moscow. The two sides found themselves playing in thick fog but the referee didn't want to abandon the game because of the distance the Soviet side had travelled, so he let play continue and the game swiftly descended into farce. One Arsenal player was sent off for fighting but sneaked back on again in the fog. The Russian side sent their substitute on – but didn't pull off one of their players and there were strong suspicions in the crowd that the Dynamos had in fact sent several other players on for good measure! The problem was, no-one could see well enough to count them. To add to the confusion, the Arsenal goalie got disorientated in the fog, ran into a goal post and concussed himself. He was replaced by a member of the crowd!

No-one really knows what the final score was but the record books say 4–3 to Dynamo. However, Arsenal still claim to this day that it was a 4–4 draw.

★　★　★

Guess what vehicles take part in the annual Twelve Mile 500 in Indiana? Powered lawnmowers. During the race, which has been run for over 30 years, participants reach nearly 30 mph on the straight. Entrants are limited to factory-built stock lawnmowers and the race begins with the cry of 'Gentlemen, start your mowers!'

★　★　★

Cricket seems to attract unusual reasons for stoppages. Apart from the well-documented streakers, a mackerel once stopped play. This happened in 1986 during a match played between the Stowe Templars and the Old Cliftonians at Bristol. The mackerel dropped from the sky, just missing the batsman's head, after being dropped by a passing seagull.

Two years later a game between Launceston and the Old Suttonians in Cornwall was interrupted by camels walking on to the wicket. They'd escaped from a nearby circus.

A match between England and Sri Lanka youth teams at the famous Colombo Cricket Club ground in 1987 was stopped

> I don't even watch pro basketball. If I had the choice of watching a pro basketball game or two mice making it on television, I'd watch the mice. Even if the screen was fuzzy.
> – Bobby Knight, US Olympic basketball coach

when a large and 'vicious-looking' iguana interrupted the game. A journalist reported that the creature 'crept menacingly' on to the pitch. After cocking its beady eyes at the English team the iguana loped off again and play re-commenced.

★　★　★

What are the odds, do you think, on a jockey starting a race on one horse – and finishing it on another? Pretty astronomical I'd say, but that's precisely what happened at a two-mile steeplechase race at Southwell race track in 1953. Jockey Mick Morrissey left the starting gate on 20–1 Knother, but crossed the finishing line on the favourite, Royal Student. At the fifth fence, Royal Student fell, throwing his rider. Knother then crashed straight into the disorientated favourite, pitching Mick Morrissey high in the air. By an incredible chance, he landed squarely in Royal Student's saddle as the horse struggled to its feet and rode him on to the finish line.

★   ★   ★

Women should keep away from the Finnish village of Sonkajarvi – unless they want to be carried across a 250-yard obstacle course consisting of tunnels, brick walls, water jumps and even blazing hoops. The village is home to the annual World Woman-Carrying Championships where Ilpo Ronkko has won the event several times. His opponents, however, have criticised him for carrying exceptionally small women. Rumours have also been flying that they weren't even women at all, but midgets in dresses.

★   ★   ★

A match in South Africa was held up when batsman Darryl Cullinan hit a six which soared heavenwards before diving straight through the ground's canteen window, landing in a pan of fried squid. Spare balls could not be found and it took ten minutes before the ball had cooled down enough to handle, and another ten for umpires to scrape off the thick coat of grease.

★   ★   ★

The new caddies on North Carolina's prestigious Talamore golf course are turning out to be very popular. They don't insist on giving you advice, don't expect tips and don't butt in on conversations with your golfing partner. The worst they do is relieve themselves on the green – but then, they are llamas. The club has found the animals to be ideal caddies and are now offering them for hire.

> I do not speak the English so good, but then I speak the driving very well.
> – Emerson Fittipaldi

At the Cherwell Edge Golf Course, Oxfordshire, club pro Joe Kingston swears by his caddie, Henry the llama. Llamas are used to carrying heavy loads and their large padded hooves spread the weight of the clubs and don't damage the turf.

*　　*　　*

In the 1936 Berlin Olympics, a furious row broke out after the women's 100 metres. The American runner Helen Stephens had defeated the Polish favourite Stella Walsh (real name Stanislawa Walasiewicz) and the rumour quickly spread that lanky six foot Helen Stephens was secretly a man.

To quash the stories, Helen submitted to a sex test and proved she was a woman. One person who was in no doubt at all that Helen was all woman was Adolf Hitler. After winning her event, Helen was invited to a personal audience with the Führer in his private box. After a few clumsy words, Helen recalled that Hitler abruptly started groping her bottom. 'You are a true Aryan type, you should be running for Germany,' he panted, presumably thinking this was rather smooth and seductive talk. He then asked her to spend a dirty weekend with him at the Berchtesgaden, but Helen turned his advances down flat before making a hurried exit.

By the way, you may be interested to know that while Helen passed the sex test, it was probably rather fortunate that defeated runner Stella Walsh was not asked to go through the same. At the time a journalist described her as having 'long man-like strides' but he didn't realise how right he was. In 1980, Stella was inadvertently caught up in a bungled robbery attempt and shot dead. An autopsy subsequently revealed *her* to be a man...

Just to add to the strangeness of the 1936 Olympics, the German high jumper Dora Ratjen turned out be a man as well.

★ ★ ★

It's important to pace yourself during a long-distance race – at
least that's what British athlete Chris Stewart believed. In a 15-
mile road race in Kenya he'd built up a steady lead after two
miles, but was amazed to see a local runner, Samson Kimowba,
rocket past him. Chris wasn't worried though. He knew his rival
would burn himself out and decided to maintain his steady pace
– until he glanced round and saw that a large rhinoceros had
crashed through undergrowth bordering the road, and was now
chasing after them...

★ ★ ★

Each year on 4 July the Great Lizard Race is held in Lovington,
New Mexico. Owners race their thoroughbred lizards down a 16-
foot ramp – and if they're not performing as they should, the
owners can give them a little encouraging tickle with a feather.

    Contestants can be disqualified for a foul, which includes
devouring their fellow lizards. Today the event is highly
organised but back in the bad old days, when the race first started
in 1976, the competition was fierce, to say the least. Entrants with
names like Lightning, Speedy, Lizardnardo and Bad to the Bone

were caged too long and ended up eating one another. That year the prize went to the lizard with the biggest appetite.

★ ★ ★

The annual Nude Olympics have taken place each year since 1965 in California. Both sexes compete naked in all events apart from the high jump, where swimming costumes are worn – mainly to avoid unpleasant injuries on the crossbar.

In 1991 a series of nude relay races were held in Gainesville, Florida. To avoid athletes getting sunburned they took place at night. (Imagine grabbing the baton, then finding out it wasn't actually the baton after all…)

★ ★ ★

In Australia in November 1969, batsman John Inverarity faced the bowler Greg Chappell. Inverarity had yet to score when one of Chappell's deliveries was deflected by a low-flying swallow on to the stumps. Chappell appealed but the umpire declared a no-ball. After his lucky escape, Inverarity went on to make 89 runs and *Wisden* couldn't pass up the chance to report, 'Duck Saved By Swallow'.

★ ★ ★

Taking their lead from the Flintstones, the Henley-on-Todd Regatta is held at Alice Springs each year. The crews' legs poke through holes in the boats' bottoms as they just run along a dried-up river bed to the finish line. The races echo the Henley-on-Thames Regatta with pairs, eights and coxless four events being held – all on the same principle.

In 1973, the race had to be cancelled, to the bitter disappointment of all competitors. The reason? Torrential rains had filled the river bed.

★ ★ ★

While all eyes were on the World Cup this year, the real sporting action was taking place over in Dublin, Georgia, where they were hosting the third Redneck Games. Designed to reflect and celebrate the lifestyle and culture of the hard-drinking, gun-toting, chain-smoking, beer-bellied all-American 'Good Ol' Boys' this one-day event offered a wide choice of events which the Olympics have somehow, inexplicably, missed out from their schedules.

The discriminating Redneck participants could choose from a wealth of different events to enter, including playing tunes on their armpits, long-distance

> If I was smart enough to be a doctor I'd be a doctor. I ain't, so I'm a football player.
> – Dick Butkus, linebacker of the Chicago Bears.

watermelon seed spitting, professional cigarette-flicking and belly flopping (into a mud pool).

If it sounds like women were being left out, don't worry. There were 'Tight Butt' and 'Big Hair' contests in which they could demonstrate their full potential.

Over 5,000 spectators got to cheer on their favourite inebriates and the winners in each event got to take home a special trophy, made out of flattened Budweiser cans.

★　★　★

Each spring, the department of mechanical engineering at the Southern Technical Institute in Marietta, Georgia, holds a bathtub derby. Cast-iron bathtubs are fitted with small motorbike engines, wheels and seats and are raced along a one-mile course, reaching speeds of 85 mph.

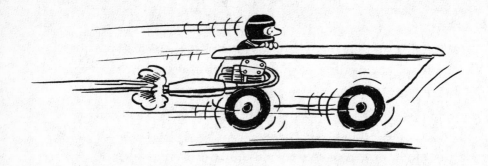

CHAPTER 10

The Sporting Hall of Shame

'Stupid, appalling, disgusting and disgraceful'
– David Coleman, commentating on the vicious
1966 World Cup match between Italy and Chile

One of the most brutal bouts in Olympic boxing history was the bantamweight fight between South Korean Byun Jong-Il and Bulgarian Aleksandr Hristov – but most of the blows weren't thrown by the fighters! During the 1988 bout in Seoul, Byun twice had a point deducted by New Zealand referee Keith Walker for head butting. Those two lost points cost him the match. As Hristov's arm was raised in victory, Byun's trainer Lee Heung-Soo came storming into the ring and punched the referee in the back. Korean boxing officials then swarmed into the ring, kicking, punching and even biting the hapless Walker. To their credit, other Olympic referees rushed to his aid, fighting off the incensed Koreans and yelling for the security guards. The guards turned up but – because they were all Korean – took the side of the officials and started laying into the referees as well. 'I acted instinctively for the love of my fatherland,' one guard said later. In all the confusion, referee Keith Walker slipped out of the ring, went straight back to his hotel, packed and caught the next flight home.

After the fighting ceased, Byun Jong-Il staged a sit-down protest in the middle of the ring. Sympathetic Koreans brought him a chair to sit on and he stayed there for a record-breaking 67-minute sulk. (The previous world record was for a sulk of 51 minutes, established by a fellow Korean, flyweight Choh Dong-Kih, at the 1964 Tokyo Games.)

★　★　★

Police broke up a brawl that started during a dominoes match in Sunderland in 1981. The contestants started fighting after it was discovered that one of them had used dominoes with removable dots.

★　★　★

The Germans aren't known to be cricket lovers so when a Sri Lankan customs official discovered six cricket balls in a German tourist's luggage in 1986, he immediately became suspicious. The cricket balls were sliced open and discovered to be packed full of cannabis. The German was arrested, although I'm not sure if he was also convicted of ball tampering.

★　★　★

While Chile were losing 1–0 to Brazil in an important 1989 World Cup qualifier, Rosemary Mello threw a flare on to the pitch which apparently injured the Chilean goalkeeper, Roberto Rojas. He was taken off the pitch with blood streaming down his face while his teammates marched off in protest.

However, all was not what it seemed. An investigation later

proved that Rojas had not been injured by the flare at all. His cuts were self-inflicted by a razor blade he had hidden in his sock, a ruse to get the game abandoned and save the team from defeat.

As a result he was banned from international football for life, while Chile were banned from competing in the next two World Cups.

As for Ms Mello, well she was invited (and accepted) the opportunity to pose naked for *Playboy*.

★　★　★

Dave Bresnahan was a catcher for the baseball team, the Williamsport Bills. In a 1987 match against rivals Reading, he threw the ball to one of his fielders in an effort to trap an opposing batsman off base – but missed and the ball headed deep into the outfield. The runner thought he was home and dry – only to be tagged out by Bresnahan who was waiting for him at home base grinning, ball in hand. No-one could understand how Bresnahan managed to get the ball back so fast, least of all the opposing player.

It turned out that Bresnahan had cheated. He'd hidden the ball in his uniform all along and the object he had thrown to his fielder was actually a potato. The authorities weren't pleased with this display of unsporting behaviour and sent him off. What's more, he was fired from the team, becoming a real estate salesman. However, the stunt Bresnahan pulled was so talked about that a year later his old team invited him back to recreate the incident in front of a capacity crowd.

> Rugby is a beastly game played by gentlemen. Soccer is a gentlemen's game played by beasts. American football is a beastly game played by beasts.
> – Harry Blaha

★ ★ ★

The 1933 Kentucky Derby went down in racing history as the 'Dirty Derby' after the exploits of two jockeys, Don Meade (riding Broker's Tip) and Herb Fisher (on Head Play). As both mounts headed neck and neck towards the finish the two jockeys tried everything they could to dismount the other. They pulled each other's saddles and then tried to push one another off. Fisher then began to hit Meade with his whip. This continued as the horses thundered down the home straight, Meade and Broker's Tip winning by a nose. Even after they'd crossed the finish line, Fisher continued to whip his opponent in full view of the crowd, even attacking him after the victory celebration.

After an investigation, both riders were suspended for 30 days – but didn't talk to one another for another 32 years.

★ ★ ★

The system of red and yellow cards was first introduced to the Football League in October 1976. George Best has the unenviable place in the record books as the very first player to be shown a red card.

★ ★ ★

Peru's national soccer team used unconventional tactics to help them overcome their opponents in an important 1998 World Cup qualifier match against Colombia – the country's top witch doctor.

" There are two types of football coaches. Them that have been fired and them that are going to be fired. "
– Bum Phillips

Medicine man Juan Osco held assorted rituals that included spitting at and hurting voodoo dolls that resembled Colombian players. All the dolls had their eyes covered up so they couldn't see the Peruvian goal and their legs bound together, to prevent them from running. The doll representing the Colombian goalkeeper even had his hands tied.

Did it work? Well, shortly before the match, Colombian midfielder Mauricio Serna went down with appendicitis – but the rest of the team stayed immune to the magic, earning an important 1–1 draw.

★   ★   ★

In September 1983 Swaziland's football association banned the use of witch doctors in helping their teams to victory. It had long been a tradition for local 'magic men' to prepare a special mixture called a 'muti' which, when painted across the goal line, would act to repel any shots. The practice was stopped, not because the football association really thought the mixture worked, but because games were interrupted when spectators – and even players – tried to remove their opponents 'muti' – by urinating in each other's goalmouths.

★   ★   ★

Anglers Joan and William Parks thought they could outwit the locals in the annual Salmon Derby held in the Washington fishing town of Port Angeles in 1981. They managed to win first and second prizes but when challenged by suspicious rivals, their lack of attention to detail let them down. For a start, when their prize-winning fish were examined they were found to be partly frozen. Secondly, it was also proved that the fish had originally been caught in fresh water.

The Port Angeles authorities took the incident seriously enough to arrest them for conspiracy to commit theft in the first degree (their prizes included a car and a boat).

After a four-day show trial, the pair were convicted and sentenced to six months in jail and banned from fishing for five years.

★ ★ ★

Everyone understood that the King of Belgium had a rather pressing schedule, so when he requested that the 10,000 metres at the 1920 Antwerp Olympic Games be brought forward from 5.50 pm to 2.15 pm the officials changed it without arguing. However, French runner Joseph Guillemot had just had an exceptionally large and filling lunch and was therefore forced to race without having time to digest his food. He did manage to come second, but then spoiled the occasion by vigorously throwing up on the winner, Paavo Nurmi.

★ ★ ★

Argentinian jockey Leopoldo Barcena could seemingly do wonders with his horses, in particular an old nag known as La Muchi. After a long period of terrible performances she won two races in quick succession at a meeting in 1960. In her next race at the Cordoba racetrack she was holding sixth position when a sudden dramatic spurt of speed enabled her to zoom past five horses in the last 200 metres to win the race.

> ❝ I wouldn't ever set out to hurt anybody deliberately unless it was, you know, important. Like a league game or something. ❞
> – Dick 'The Animal' Buktus, linebacker of the Chicago Bears

Officials thought something was wrong with La Muchi's electrifying performance. It was. Under her saddle they found apparatus rigged up to give the horse a 100-volt shock whenever her jockey made contact with his spurs.

Barcena was eventually arrested and, appropriately enough, charged…

★   ★   ★

Champion bridge players Lawrence Cohen and Richard Katz were forced to withdraw from the 1977 US Bridge team trials when it was alleged they were cheating. The *New York Times* reported that the two players used a complicated series of sniffs, coughs, wheezes and croaks to pass bidding messages to each other.

In the same year the American Contract Bridge League expelled two Florida players after it was discovered that they had used the positions of their pencils on the table to indicate which cards a player wanted his partner to lead.

★   ★   ★

Trainer Piero Pucci coached an all-girl football team in Foggia, Italy, but faced a big problem just before a crucial cup match when his regular goalkeeper failed to turn up. There were no substitutes good enough to play in goal so Piero did what any other red-blooded football-loving fan would do – he put on women's clothing and took her place. Wearing a wig, and a bra filled with two ripe watermelons, Piero took to the pitch and

> What I said to them at half-time would be unprintable on the radio.
> – Gerry Francis

119

performed admirably, even saving a penalty. Trouble came in the second half though, when Piero punched one of his opponents, shouting in a very deep voice, 'Back off, bitch'. His cover was blown, literally, after one of the watermelons exploded after he clashed with a striker.

He was ordered off by the referee, who admitted later that he found Piero 'attractive, in a homely sort of way'. When asked if he ever suspected that the goalkeeper was, in fact, a man, the ref said that Piero's hairy legs were 'not that unusual for a buxom country girl who had grown up in the hills tending sheep'.

✦ ✦ ✦

It was obvious to everyone that the World Cup match between West Germany and Austria in 1982 was not being played competitively. The West Germans won 1–0 – which was just the score needed for both teams to progress into the second round at the expense of Algeria. The French national coach Michel Hidalgo was so disgusted that he later publicly commented, 'Both teams played with such lack of aggression they should win the Nobel Peace Prize!'

✦ ✦ ✦

Snooker player Alex 'Hurricane' Higgins has managed to upset one or two opponents in his turbulent career. On one occasion he played Norman Squire, a 63-year-old Australian snooker champ, in a 1973 exhibition match in Sydney. Not quite gracious in victory, after the match Higgins allegedly said that Squire was 'nothing but an old has-been'. This resulted in him being hauled out of the club and made to sit in the gutter outside while he wrote an apology on a piece of toilet paper.

Another time he lost to Graham Miles at a tournament in

Wales, calling his opponent a 'jammy bald bugger'. The ensuing punch-up was also not a good advertisement for the sport.

> ❛ If I'd known I was going to be fined for that, I'd really have let him have it.
> – John McEnroe, after being fined in the US Open for calling the umpire a 'fat turd' ❜

One challenge that Higgins definitely enjoyed was put to him by fellow hell-raiser Oliver Reed. He invited Higgins to his house for a weekend tournament of snooker, table tennis, arm wrestling and – wait for it – disco dancing. It's not recorded who won (or if anyone remembers winning).

✳   ✳   ✳

Ricky Goddard of North Warnborough had a disciplinary record that makes Vinnie Jones look like a softie. By 1992 he had been suspended for five out of his nine years as a footballer including a six-month ban for sneaking into the ref's changing room at half-time and urinating all over his clothes.

✳   ✳   ✳

Major Boris Onischenko was a member of the Russian pentathlon team at the 1976 Montreal Olympics who was disqualified for some high-tech cheating. In the fencing event it was noticed that he managed to score hits on his opponents without even seemingly touching them. His sword was taken away for investigation where it was discovered that it featured a concealed switch which, when pushed, registered a hit for him.

The major was sent home in disgrace from the Games, exiled to Siberia and ended up managing a fish shop in Kiev.

★ ★ ★

Chinese Premier Mao Tse-tung claimed to have smashed a world swimming record – at the age of 72. In July 1966, he told his people that he had swum a ten-mile stretch of the Yangtze in under an hour proving that if he was fit enough to tackle the notorious river he was also still fit enough to rule his country. It was only after his death that his personal doctor dared to pour scorn on Mao's world record. 'Mao was a chronic chain smoker and far too fat even to swim a few feet,' he said. 'If he only completed a small part of the journey as he claims – which I don't believe – it was because he accidentally fell in and got swept along by the current.'

★ ★ ★

Doc Kearns, the manager of heavyweight champ Jack Dempsey, had his own version of the 'horseshoe in a boxing glove' trick. Before a championship fight in 1919, Kearns placed a $10,000 bet on his man knocking out rival Jess Willard in the first round (at odds of 10–1). But in an attempt to ensure he won his $100,000, he pulled off a stunt that he only revealed almost 50 years later. Dempsey himself claimed he knew nothing about it.

Just before the fight, Kearns filled a talcum powder tin with plaster of Paris and told his trainers to wet and powder Dempsey's bandages before they put his gloves on. This was, he claimed, to 'keep his hands comfortable' in the 100-degree heat. Of course, the water made the plaster harden so it's not surprising that Willard claimed that it felt like he was being hit by blocks of concrete.

He was knocked down several times in that first round. Kearns said that 'every punch landed with the hollow sound of a mallet crunching into watermelon'. Despite the onslaught,

Willard survived the round and Kearns lost his bet. Not surprisingly, Dempsey won the fight after Willard threw in the towel at the start of round three.

When the truth did eventually come out in Kearns' 1964 memoirs Willard was philosophical about his defeat saying, 'As long as I got robbed, I'm glad I got robbed by the best man in the country at stealing.'

★ ★ ★

Ferrari driver Eddie Irvine is well known among the motor-racing fraternity for playing pranks. On one occasion in 1996 he was being interviewed by pit lane reporter Tony Jardine after yet another Ferrari breakdown. It was an intense, eye-to-eye live interview and all credit must be given to Jardine's professionalism. You see, throughout the interview, while Jardine kept a straight face and continued asking questions, Irvine was slowly emptying a bottle of ice-cold water down the unruffled reporter's trousers.

* * *

In November 1984 the French third division rugby side Vergt decided to protest at the suspension of four players. During their game against rivals Gujan Mestras they deliberately played with four players short, refused to compete for possession of the ball or offer any opposition whatsoever. This resulted in a record loss of 236–0. (Being a side to stick to their principles, their protest continued in the next game. This time they broke their own record, losing 350–0).

* * *

We all think that Queen Boadicea led a heroic resistance movement against the Roman invaders in the first century AD, but the truth is somewhat less glamorous. Boadicea got on quite well with the Romans. She even got a personal loan from the Roman philosopher Seneca to indulge her passion for horse racing and to build a fine stable. Unfortunately, Seneca had the temerity to ask her to pay him back. Outraged, Boadicea declared war on the Romans and the rest is history.

* * *

After a furious fight erupted on the pitch between Mike Flanagan and Derek Hales, the referee had no option but to send them both off. This left Charlton Athletic down to nine men. Flanagan and Hales were supposedly both on the same team!

In a very similar incident, Blackburn Rovers midfielder David Batty was

> I went to a fight the other night and an ice hockey game broke out.
> – Rodney Dangerfield

124

cautioned for fighting with his own teammate, Graeme Le Saux, during a televised match with Spartak Moscow in November 1995.

★ ★ ★

Who do you think holds the record for the fastest-ever booking in English football? No it's not Gary Lineker but Vinnie Jones, booked after just five seconds in a match between Sheffield United and Manchester City.

★ ★ ★

Fernando d'Ercoli was playing for Pianta against Arpax in an Italian amateur league game in 1989 when he was given the red card. He was so incensed that he snatched it from the ref's hand and ate it.

Similarly, when Mike Bagley of Bristol was booked for swearing in January 1984 he stole the referee's notebook, ripped out the page with his name on and ate it.

★ ★ ★

Chess grand masters kicking each other? Just what is the world coming to? This ungentlemanly behaviour took place in 1977 when Viktor Korchnoi played Tigran Petrosian. The two players were notable enemies and what started as simple 'chess board knocking' to put each other off soon degenerated as Viktor and Tigran lashed out at each

> ❝ The sound of the ball hitting the batsman's skull was music to my ears. ❞
> – Jeff Thomson

other under the table. The only way tournament organisers could get the players to stop was by separating their feet and legs by a large wooden board.

★　★　★

Alex Hay and Henry Cotton were commentating at a Colgate Ladies Tournament at Sunningdale. 'That's a beautiful looking hole, don't you think?' asked Alex Hay describing the seventeenth. 'Yes,' replied Henry Cotton, adding, 'but it was a lot tighter in my day.' Nothing wrong with that you might think – except the picture being seen by TV viewers at the time was the backside of shapely American golfer Marlene Floyd.

CHAPTER 11

The Good Old Days

'To hell with Babe Ruth!'
– Japanese battle cry in World War Two

**I hope that every Jap that mentions my name gets shot,
and to hell with all Japs anyway!**
– Babe Ruth

The bloodiest event in modern sporting history took place in 1903. It was the infamous Paris–Madrid motorcar rally. Some 216 drivers set off over the 870-mile course, competing for the new 'Auto Championship of the World'. Of course, cars were still a novelty in 1903 and many people had never seen one before. Consequently, thousands of spectators turned up to line the route – that is, thousands of people who had never seen a car before and who had no idea how dangerous it was to step in front of one. There was carnage for 300 miles. To get a better view, spectators would often stand right in the middle of the road. Drivers had the unenviable choice of hitting them and mowing them down or swerving into the crowd by the roadside. Other drivers, stunned by the accidents unfolding in front of them, lost control and skidded into other cars or into the spectators. The police finally called an emergency halt to the race at Bordeaux after only 343 miles. By that time 550 people had been killed and thousands more injured…

★ ★ ★

What does it mean when you say that a cricketer is 'out for a duck'? Why a duck? Why not 'out for a rhinoceros' or 'out for a sheep', for example? The reason, apparently, is that the number '0' resembles a duck's egg in shape. Hence 'out for a duck'. Equally, you might want to ask why we say 'fifteen–love' in tennis. Why not 'fifteen – lust' or 'fifteen – infatuation'? It so happens that the term 'love' is a corruption of the French word 'l'oeuf' which means the egg, which we all know is shaped like the number '0'. So tennis commentators are actually saying 'fifteen – egg'.

* * *

The first proper sporting fixture to be televised by the BBC was boxing from the Alexander Amateur Boxing Club, on 6 November 1931. The only words of advice given to early BBC sports commentators were 'don't swear'.

Incidentally, in 1939, the *New York Times* concluded that sport would never be popular on television…

* * *

Do you know why golf courses have eighteen holes? Well, the famous St Andrews golf course in Scotland was laid out with 19 holes (not including the bar). The club then decided to get rid of one of them so they could lengthen the remaining eighteen holes. All other golf courses then followed suit.

* * *

When World War One broke out in 1914, there was outrage as English football clubs decided to carry on with their season. A leading historian writing in *The Times* thundered, 'we view with indignation and alarm the persistence of association football clubs in doing their best for the enemy. Every club that employs a professional football player is bribing a much needed recruit to refrain from enlistment, and every spectator who pays his gate money is contributing so much to German victory.' The Dean of Lincoln expressed his disgust with spectators, calling them 'onlookers who, while so many of their fellow men are giving themselves in their country's peril, still go gazing at football'.

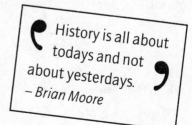

History is all about todays and not about yesterdays.
– Brian Moore

Concern was raised in Parliament that workers in munitions factories were thinking about football rather than on the job in hand which was why, they said, so many British artillery shells were failing to explode. Matches were banned in the vicinity of the factories. At the so-called Khaki Cup Final, Lord Derby presented the cup and announced before the capacity crowd, 'You have played with one another and against one another for the cup. It is now the duty of everyone to join with each other and play a sterner game – for England.'

The criticism was ill-founded. A Footballers' Battalion – the 17 Service Battalion of the Middlesex Regiment – was formed and at Stamford Bridge there were large posters saying, 'Do you want to be a Chelsea die-hard? Join the 17 Battalion of the Middlesex Regiment and follow the lead given by your favourite football players!' By 1915, the FA claimed they had helped to recruit half a million men for the war effort.

The Asian game of mah-jongg was actually named and copyrighted by an American, Joe P Babcock, who lived in Shanghai in the early 1900s. It takes its name from the mythical bird that appears on one of the tiles. Babcock introduced the game to California in the 1920s where its popularity swept the state – and then the rest of the country. The craze reached a peak in 1923 then died, like most fads, as quickly as it grew. What did dedicated mah-jong players forsake their tiles for? The sudden popularity of the crossword puzzle.

* * *

We all take televised action replays for granted but in 1963, the first one was shown on American TV during the annual Army vs

Navy football match. A
touchdown by the Army
was shown again seconds
later accompanied by the
commentator shouting
for the benefit of
confused viewers, 'This
is not live! The Army
did not, repeat, did not, just
score again!' (Incidentally, it was the BBC who installed
the first action-replay machine in the UK, in 1968.)

Did you know?

President Teddy Roosevelt lost
an eye while boxing and saved
American football from being
banned, despite personally
detesting the sport.

★ ★ ★

The 1872 Football Association Challenge Cup was the first
recognised cup event in football history. The favourites were
Glasgow club Queen's Park who had effectively invented a new
football tactic called 'passing the ball'. However, the team had no
money and had to depend on public subscriptions to afford to
come down to London to play Wanderers in the semi-final. The
match ended in a 0–0 draw and, as the Scottish players didn't
have enough money for board and lodgings in London, they had
to forfeit the replay. In the end the cup was won by Wanderers,
with their star player the Reverend RWS Vidal, nicknamed 'The
Prince of Dribblers', setting up the only goal of the match. The
18-inch-high silver cup was received by team captain CW Alcock,
who just happened to be Secretary of the Football Association
and the prime instigator of the competition in the first place.

★ ★ ★

I can hardly believe it myself, but overarm bowling in cricket was
originally invented by a woman.

Originally, bowlers bowled underarm as in the sport of bowls, which is how bowling got its name. The woman who changed the face of cricket forever was the sister of Victorian cricketer John Willes. Willes used to like to practise at home, with his sister as bowler. However, the huge billowing skirts Victorian women wore at the time made it exceptionally difficult for her to bowl underarm. She tried bowling over her shoulder to keep her arm away from her skirt – and gave her brother no end of problems in trying to hit the ball. Realising that overarm bowling was much harder to bat against than the conventional underarm delivery, Willes went on to introduce his sister's invention to the game with devastating effect. In no time at all, his style of delivery was taken up by bowlers everywhere.

★ ★ ★

According to popular sporting legend, the noble art of hurdling was invented at Exeter College in 1850. Some well-to-do students had hired local horses for an impromptu point-to-point event, but found the horses so hopeless at jumping that they decided to dismount and jump the fences themselves!

★ ★ ★

In 1863, the Football Association was created in the Freemasons' Tavern in Lincoln's Inn Fields. On the agenda were the rules for the game drawn up in Sheffield in 1857. The need for a new set of rules was clear, as there were two different factions in the game – 'the dribblers' and 'the handlers'. One preferred kicking the ball while the other preferred to carry it.

The new association weren't impressed by the Sheffield rules,

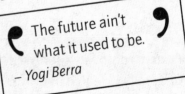

The future ain't what it used to be.
– Yogi Berra

saying that they still allowed for some unsportsmanlike behaviour on the pitch, and quickly drew up some amendments which included 'no player shall be allowed to wear projecting nails…from his boots' and 'no player shall be held and hacked at the same time'! However, a number of the clubs still wanted to allow players to run with the ball and to be able to 'charge, hold, trip or hack' opposing players. After two months of heated discussions, the association split, with dissenters moving away in favour of rugby instead, which got its own association in 1871.

Interestingly, until 1867 you weren't allowed to pass the ball forward in football, just as in rugby.

★　★　★

Sir Arthur Conan Doyle is best known as the creator of Sherlock Holmes but he was quite a sporting hero. In addition to being a county footballer he was an international racing driver and played cricket for the MCC, once bowling out WG Grace.

★　★　★

In 1895, the British Ladies Football Club was formed, much to the chagrin of the Football Association. They played their first match in Crouch End in North London the same year in front of an impressive 10,000 spectators, wearing a kit comprising heavy-duty knee-length sensible skirts, thick and heavy shinpads and large droopy nightcaps.

★　★　★

We might so easily have been placing bets on 'The Bunbury' instead of the Derby today if it hadn't been for the toss of a coin. Both the twelfth Earl of Derby and Sir Charles Bunbury wanted to put their name to the event in 1780. Sensibly, rather than fighting a duel, the two men decided to settle it by tossing a coin. Incidentally The Oaks race is named after the Earl of Derby's house.

✦　✦　✦

Take a look at your trousers. Chances are, they're designed like that because of the 1896 Derby! The 1896 race was won by a racehorse named Persimmon, owned by Edward, Prince of Wales. After the victory, the prince ignored royal protocol and excitedly jumped out of the royal box to go and congratulate his jockey. However, since the going was soft, to avoid ruining his trousers in the mud, the Prince quickly turned up the bottoms. The very next day, everyone who was anyone in London was turning up their trouser bottoms too. The fashion craze spread until the turn-up was commonplace all over the world.

✦　✦　✦

Braveheart didn't tell the full story. In 1457, the Scottish Parliament had to rush through emergency measures to ban the game of golf because Highland warriors were spending too much time playing the game instead of honing their fighting skills for use against the 'Sassenachs'!

✦　✦　✦

Despite the fact that boxing was still illegal and technically 'a breach of the peace' in this country in 1860, Farnborough in Hampshire played host to the first world title fight. At the ringside were Charles Dickens and William Thackeray, numerous judges and clergymen and so many MPs that critics claimed that the fight had 'emptied the Houses of Parliament'. The two title contestants were the Englishman Tom Sayers and a huge

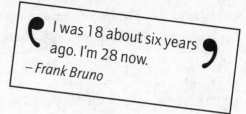

I was 18 about six years ago. I'm 28 now.
– Frank Bruno

American brute of a man called John 'The Benecia Boy' Heenan. They started fighting at 7.30 in the morning and battled away for a bloody 37 rounds. At this point the American had broken one of his hands and both eyes were swollen so badly he could barely see. Sayers was drenched in blood and had completely lost the use of his right arm. Neither could fight any more – but the crowd weren't about to accept that. They cut the ropes and swarmed into the ring, prodding and shoving the fighters and taunting them to fight on. The referee tried to restore order but then fled for his life as the crowd turned on him. The American fighter also had to make a run for it, pursued by a jingoistic mob yelling anti-American insults. The fight was declared a draw.

★ ★ ★

The term 'football' can be traced back as far as the fifteenth century, when it was applied to a game alternatively called 'kicking-camp' or – more sinisterly – 'savage-camp'. In the game, teams of several hundred on each side would attempt to kick a pig's bladder filled with dry peas across a pitch that could be anything up to several miles long! Games between rival villages were commonplace, and often saw 'off-the-ball incidents' like mass punch-ups breaking out. Few players had any idea where the ball was at any given time – and fewer cared. However, some form of football is almost certainly older than that. In 1314, spoilsport King Edward II issued a strict proclamation forbidding people to 'hustle over large balls' in the streets of the

City of London. The game could in fact go all the way back to Roman times, when a game called 'harpastum' which sounds quite similar in many ways was played, although historians don't know much about it. Let's hope this isn't true – otherwise the next time you sing the line 'Football's coming home' you may inadvertently be cheering on the Italians.

* * *

Ever wondered where the phrase 'back to square one' comes from? It's an old BBC Radio sports commentators term. BBC Radio first broadcast from a football match at Highbury in January 1927. To help listeners follow what was going on, the *Radio Times* that week featured a map of the pitch divided up into little numbered squares. The commentator would then tell listeners that the ball was in 'square two' or 'square four'...

* * *

The term 'hat trick' doesn't come from football. It actually comes from cricket. Back in Victorian times, if a bowler took three wickets on successive balls, some clubs rewarded him with a new hat!

* * *

Chess originated in the Muslim world and came to Britain with the Normans. Interestingly, the original Arabian version had no queen, because of Islamic attitudes towards women. Instead the piece was called a 'Vizier' or 'Advisor'. Bishops weren't mullahs though. They were originally elephants.

CHAPTER 12

Brain Over Brawn

'The secret of managing a baseball team is to keep the five guys who hate you away from the five who are undecided'
– *Casey Stengel*

Bare-faced cheek can be every bit as important as skill or nerve in motor racing. In the 1930 Mille Miglia competition, Alfa Romeo driver Tazio Nuvolari was trailing behind the Maserati of Achille Varzi and there seemed little hope of catching him. The last part of the race, however, was run in darkness – giving Nuvolari an ingenious idea. He switched his car headlights off as he drove. Looking back in his rear-view mirror, Varzi found he could no longer see the Alfa Romeo's lights and assumed he'd fallen well behind. This made him ease up and relax. The next thing he knew, Nuvolari's Alfa Romeo came hurtling past him in the darkness to take the flag!

★　★　★

When the celebrated jockey Sir Gordon Richards lined up on his mount Ridgewood for the start of the 13-furlong Midland St

Leger Trial Stakes in 1949, he was under strict instructions from his trainer, Noel Murless, not to take the lead straight off, but to wait until the third furlong post.

Little did Sir Gordon know, however, that the only other horse and rider in the race, Tommy Lowrey riding Courier, had been given precisely the same instruction! The race began – and neither horse moved a muscle. Finally, the starter sent an assistant over to crack a whip and both horses moved off under tight rein at what can best be described as a very slow canter. The crowd jeered as the two dawdling jockeys took a minute and a half to reach the first furlong marker, which is normally about the time it takes to run over half the race. Then, at the third furlong marker, both jockeys suddenly cut loose as instructed. Sir Gordon eventually won by three lengths but the race – if you could call it that – had taken almost twice as long as usual to complete.

★ ★ ★

During World War Two world heavyweight champion Joe Louis served in the US Army as a truck driver. One day, he got into a minor scrape with another truck. The other driver leaped down from his cab and harangued Louis, calling him every name under the sun – not having any idea who he was threatening. Throughout the whole thing, Louis just sat in his seat and didn't do anything. After the other driver had stormed off, Louis' companion in the truck wanted to know why the boxer hadn't pulverised the other driver. 'Why should I?' Louis replied. 'When someone insulted Caruso, did he sing an aria for him?'

Another story often told about Louis concerns his fight against 'Two Ton' Tony Galento. 'Two Ton Tony' wasn't supposed to have a chance, but early on in the fight he caught Louis with a crushing left hook and sent the champion sprawling on the canvas. Almost immediately, Louis was up again before the referee had even started the count. At the end of the round, his trainer, Jack Blackburn, told him off in no uncertain terms. 'Joe,' he said, 'you're supposed to take a count when that happens. Why didn't you stay down for nine like I always told you?' 'What – and let him get all that rest?' Louis retorted.

★ ★ ★

They take their football seriously in Catanzaro in Italy so when, during a game between the home side and Palermo, the score was precariously balanced at 1–1 with little time remaining, it was a brave referee indeed who'd disallow a penalty for the home team. On this occasion, however, the match referee did. And, to add insult to injury, he then disallowed a second penalty. Tempers were running hot by the time the final whistle blew and the referee had to sprint off the pitch and out of a side entrance as fans swept out of the stands baying for his blood. The fans were so incensed that they kept on chasing the referee through the streets, until he managed to give them the slip by diving into a restaurant. Exhausted, he decided to dine at the restaurant, but he had just received his first course when the restaurant owner – a keen soccer fan – returned from the match and recognised him. He unceremoniously threw the hapless referee out of his trattoria, throwing a few choice words and a bowl of soup after him.

For the referee, this was the last straw. He'd had enough. It was time for revenge. He went to the nearest public telephone booth and rang up the restaurant, saying he was Catanzaro's manager and the entire team would be dropping by the restaurant that night to

> Yes. I swear a lot. But as I've played in several countries I can choose which language I like.
> – Jurgen Klinsmann

eat. He then rang the Catanzaro ground claiming to be the restaurant owner. He was outraged about the match, he said. By way of consolation, the restaurant would be honoured if the entire team would eat and dine there that night for just a token few lire. Naturally, the manager readily accepted.

So, as the referee looked on from a safe vantage point, the entire Catanzaro side turned up at the restaurant, all with hearty appetites, and proceeded to eat and drink the very finest food, wines and spirits the trattoria could offer. Innocently, the restaurant manager then presented them with the bill. Anarchy ensued almost immediately. Confused debate quickly turned into mindless violence. The team rioted and wrecked the entire restaurant while the owner and the Catanzaro manager rolled over and over on the floor, punching and biting each other. The referee slipped away just as the first of the police vans started pulling up...and the hapless manager was hauled away and charged with assault.

★　★　★

Flying from Washington to New York, Muhammad Ali was giving the airline stewardess a hard time, refusing to do up his seatbelt as requested. 'Sister,' he said, staring straight at her, 'Superman don't need no seat belt!' To which the stewardess replied, as quick as a flash, 'Superman don't need no plane either!'

★　★　★

In the early 1970s, the American Olympic hammer-throwing team completely destroyed the morale of their Soviet opponents before the big event. They shared a practice field with the Russians and, when they had the field to themselves, the Americans made fake hammer landing marks at impossibly huge

Muhammed Ali:

'I'm a great golfer. I just haven't played the game yet.'

'I'm so fast I could hit you before God gets the news.'

'When you're as great as I am, it's hard to be humble.'

'It's just a job. Grass grows. Birds fly. Waves pound the sand. I beat people up.'

'I'm not only the greatest, I'm the double greatest.'

'I'll beat him so bad he'll need a shoehorn to put his hat on.'

'I've seen him shadow-boxing – and the shadow won.'
– *on George Foreman*

'I like your show and I like your style.
But your pay's so bad I won't be back for a while!'
– *to Michael Parkinson*

'Look at me! Am I not beauty? Inhale me, am I not perfume?'
– *addressing the crowd in Louisville welcoming him back after his Olympic boxing victory*

'Joe Frazier's so ugly, they ought to donate his face to the World Wildlife Fund.'

'He's so ugly that when he cries, the tears run down the back of his head.'
– *on Sonny Liston*

'I've wrestled with an alligator
I've tussled with a whale
I've done handcuffed lightnin'
And thrown thunder in jail.'

distances from the starting point. The Russians discovered the marks, and panicked when they found their best athletes could get nowhere near them...

Players at the Waika golf club in Hawaii were subject to a terrible delay caused by four Japanese golfers. They were so inexperienced (never having set foot on a golf course before) that three of them soon lost their balls. They hadn't brought spares along so they continued with the one remaining ball using an ingenious method.

The first player would hit the ball, mark where it landed and then run back so the second player could hit his shot – and so on until all four players had finished that hole.

By the end of the 1890 FA Cup Final, Blackburn Rovers had won two things. The first was the FA Cup itself, after defeating Sheffield Wednesday 6–0. The second was the 'best-dressed team award'. Due to a clash of colours with their opponents, Blackburn had to resort to wearing the evening-dress shirts they had brought with them for a reception after the match.

In a bid to give themselves an extra 'edge', sports professionals are increasingly turning towards 'alternative' therapies and one of the most popular is hypnosis to boost the confidence. Does it work? Well, Frank Bruno underwent hypnosis before his fight with Mike Tyson, and in 1949, the entire Hinckley Athletic soccer team was hypnotised before their match against Bedworth Town.

Like Bruno, they lost.
While competing in the
1956 Australian National
Swimming
Championships, Gary
Winran had himself

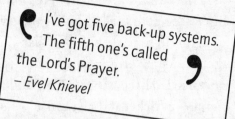

I've got five back-up systems. The fifth one's called the Lord's Prayer.
– Evel Knievel

hypnotised to be convinced that he was being
chased down the pool by a ferocious great white shark! He only
managed second place, so we can only speculate on what the
winner believed was chasing him!

Taking inspiration from the Bible, American hurdler Forrest
Smithson ran the 110 metres hurdles at the 1908 London
Olympics holding the good book in his left hand. It must have
helped because he won the gold medal, winning by five yards.

* * *

When Norm van Brocklin, a famous NFL quarterback and coach,
underwent brain surgery in 1979, there were persistent rumours
that he would have to retire from football altogether. However,
Norm soon proved himself as sharp as ever. When reporters
pestered him for details of his operation, he said, 'It was a brain
transplant. I got a sports writer's brain so I could be sure that I
got one that hadn't been used!'

* * *

When Gerhard Berger and Ayrton Senna became teammates at
McLaren, many thought there would be fireworks. Berger was a
notorious practical joker while Senna was always serious.

One day, for no apparent reason, Berger threw Senna's briefcase out of the helicopter they were both travelling in. Senna took this in remarkably good fashion and seemed to forget about the incident. Nothing happened for a few weeks, until Berger next needed his passport. He found it in his case along with his money, air ticket and insurance – the trouble was, they had all been glued solidly together. Senna owned up but said he was just trying to be helpful; it was to prevent Berger forgetting anything.

★ ★ ★

Sir Winston Churchill was a lot sportier in his youth than might be imagined, but one game he could never warm to was golf. 'An ineffectual attempt to direct an uncontrollable sphere into an inaccessible hole with instruments ill adapted to the purpose' was how he chose to describe it.

★ ★ ★

Throughout the 1938–39 season, Sheffield United had won most of their away matches but had played appallingly at home at Bramall Lane. With three home matches left to secure promotion to Division One, manager Ted Davison used psychology to improve his team's performance, by making players think they were playing away.

Each Saturday morning before these home games the players were picked up by the team coach and driven to Derby where they had lunch. They were then driven back to Bramall Lane for the match.

The plan worked. United won two and drew one of these matches and so went up.

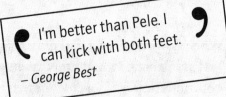

I'm better than Pele. I can kick with both feet.
– George Best

★　★　★

When a show dolphin swallowed a piece of metal and its condition started to deteriorate, California vets were stumped. They didn't have any tools suitable for retrieving it from the stomach, and didn't want to risk a surgical procedure. Instead, they plumped for an unorthodox cure in the form of Golden State Warrior's basketball player Clifford Ray. Ray, with his incredible 3 foot 3 inch arms was able to reach right down inside the dolphin and retrieve the metal.

★　★　★

Olympic swimming gold medallist Johnny Weissmuller went on to play Tarzan in no fewer than 12 movies – but his biggest challenge came on a golf course in Cuba in 1959. He was on his way to take part in a celebrity golf tournament in Havana when he and some friends were captured by Fidel Castro's guerrillas,

looking to take some rich
American hostages. The
situation was tense.
Weissmuller found himself
staring down half a dozen
rifle barrels. Then he

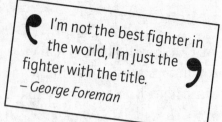

I'm not the best fighter in the world, I'm just the fighter with the title.
– George Foreman

suddenly started beating his chest and letting
out his familiar blood-curdling Tarzan yell. The guerrillas stared
at him in absolute silence and then dropped their guns and
clustered around him crying 'Tarzan! Tarzan! Welcome to Cuba,'
and begging for his autograph. After a few minutes of frantic
handshaking and autograph signing, the guerrillas gave up all
thought of taking Weissmuller and his party hostage and instead
gave them a personal armed escort to the golf tournament!

✴   ✴   ✴

Motor-racing commentators in Australia used to have a bizarre
system of keeping tabs on where the various cars were. Sharing the
spacious commentary box with them would be spotters – men
dressed similarly, each with a number on his back – one for every
car. At the start of the race, each spotter started in the grid position
of his car. Each time there was a change in the order of drivers, the
spotters changed places accordingly, jostling their way into the
new position. That way, just by looking at them, the commentator
could see at a glance that car number 6 was ahead of car number
12, which was being closely pressed by car number 2.

I wonder what happened if there was a crash or a collision?

✴   ✴   ✴

In February 1964, the then Cassius Clay took the world
heavyweight championship from Sonny Liston in a blistering

display of power and skill. Interviewing Liston on his chat show later, Michael Parkinson kindly tried to reassure him by saying, 'For a while during that fight I thought you had him scared.' Liston was quiet for a moment and then replied, 'Yeah – that's when he thought he'd killed me.'

★ ★ ★

American drivers Carroll Shelby and Dale Duncan were driving an Allard sports car in the 1954 Buenos Aires 1,000-kilometre race when a small fire broke out during a routine pit stop. With no fire extinguishers to hand, Duncan had to improvise. He put the fire out by urinating on it.

★ ★ ★

British Formula One driver Alan Stacey concealed a secret handicap. He had an artificial right leg which would have ruled him out of racing – if anyone had ever found out. At the time, in the 1950s, all drivers racing in Europe had to undergo a pre-race medical. Part of this involved testing reflexes by banging a rubber mallet on the drivers' knees – both of them.

Stacey got through the test in a cunning way. His left leg would test OK but just before his right, artificial leg was going to be tapped, one of his associates would contrive to knock something over in the surgery. When the doctor was distracted, Stacey would re-cross his legs, with the left one uppermost – again.

He got away with this trick all his racing career.

★   ★   ★

Most people were confused by Eric Cantona's philosophising, but what would they have made of American golfer Mac O'Grady? He was once asked by a journalist, 'How did that 65 compare with your 62 in the Greater Harford Open?' Mac pondered for a moment then replied, 'If I can bring the ship home with cargo and crew intact through the hurricane of the last day, that's an achievement, right?' Quite!

> We definitely will be improved this year. Last year we lost ten games. This year we only scheduled nine.
> – Ray Jenkins, coach of the Montana State football team

CHAPTER 13

Brains in Their Boots

**'A lot of boxing promoters couldn't match
the cheeks on their buttocks'**
– Mickey Duff

In 1934, Ray 'Snooks' Dowd scored the longest touchdown in American football history – by accident. He was playing in a real grudge match between his team LeHigh University and their arch-rivals, Lafayette. The game became increasingly heated and violent and Dowd took more than his share of knocks. Dazed and confused, and finding himself holding the ball, Dowd set off for goal. Unfortunately, it was his own goal he was heading towards. Just as he crossed the line, he started to understand why the crowd were bellowing at him and, without stopping, circled the end zone and reversed his run, racing the entire length of the field back again to score the winner for LeHigh! Dowd's run was a total of 210 yards!

★　★　★

At the start of his career American football star William 'The Refrigerator' Perry weighed 290 pounds. However, when his

weight hit 330 pounds, his coach decided to put him on a special diet consisting only of milk and bananas. The Refrigerator continued to pile on the weight though, because unfortunately the coach hadn't specified just how many bananas and how much milk he could consume and the player gorged himself on them, thinking he was eating himself slim…

★ ★ ★

Ralph Walton, the American boxer, is in the record books for the wrong reason. He was knocked out just eleven seconds into a fight – and ten of those seconds included the referee's count. It happened in a fight in Lewiston, Maine in 1946. The bell went for round one but Ralph was still adjusting his gumshield (tricky wearing boxing gloves) when his opponent, Al Couture, threw his KO punch.

Harvey Gartley holds a similar record in the Boxing

> If a kid wants to be a fighter, you know right away he ain't smart.
> – Anonymous boxer, 1956

Hall of Shame. He managed to knock himself out – after just 50 seconds of a bantamweight fight in Michigan in 1977. Unlike Ralph Walton, Harvey got off to a promising start, bobbing and weaving, ducking and diving around his opponent Dennis Outlette, trying to psyche him out. He dummied, shimmied to the left, leaned to the right and then threw an almighty punch. Trouble was, it missed and Ralph fell to the canvas exhausted, where he was counted out.

★ ★ ★

Journalists who don't do their research beforehand can be the bane of a sports player's life. Bill Toomey, America's 1968 decathlon Olympic gold-medal winner, once sat down with a journalist from one of America's most prestigious newspapers. 'OK,' she asked him, pen posed over notebook. 'So how far can you actually throw a decathlon?'

★ ★ ★

The 1978 World Cup semi-final between Holland and Italy was the most eventful match in Dutch player Ernie Brandt's career. In the course of the match he scored a goal – but then also managed to score an own goal and knock his own goalkeeper unconscious.

★ ★ ★

During the 1932 Olympics in Los Angeles, all the competitors in the 3000-metres steeplechase accidentally ran an extra lap due to a bizarre mix-up by the officials. American runner Joseph McCluskey lost his silver medal after being overtaken by Britain's Thomas Evenson on the 'accidental lap', but sportingly did not lodge a complaint and settled for bronze.

★ ★ ★

Abd-El Kader Zaag had been going quite well in the 1950 Tour de France but started to flag under the intense heat on the Perpignan–Nimes stage of the race. He needed refreshment so when he saw one of the spectators lining the route drinking from a bottle of wine he stopped. The bottle was gladly offered but what started off as a quick swig ended up with Abd-El refusing to give the bottle back and drinking the whole thing. Not surprisingly, he was in no fit state to carry on so he rested for a while to sober up. Shortly afterwards, feeling re-energised, he got back in the saddle and pedalled off again – in the direction he had just come from.

★ ★ ★

Legendary comedians Buddy Hackett and Jimmy 'The Schnoz' Durante were playing golf, and Durante was having a particularly bad game, his score well over 200. At the end, he asked Hackett what he should give his caddy. 'Your clubs,' Hackett replied.

★ ★ ★

At the 1964 Tokyo Olympics, the winner of the marathon was the Ethiopian Abebe Bikila, even though he'd undergone an appendectomy only 40 days beforehand.
Abebe had won the 1960 marathon in Rome – and in bare feet, to cap it all – but despite this the Japanese band at the medal ceremony were completely

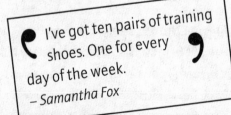

I've got ten pairs of training shoes. One for every day of the week.
– Samantha Fox

unprepared and had no idea what the Ethiopian national anthem sounded like – or even if there was one. So, as Abebe received his medal, the band played the Japanese national anthem instead – which confused no end of spectators…

Officials at the 1952 Olympics in Helsinki were equally red-faced after the men's 1500 metres final. The event was won by an outsider, Josef Bartel, from Luxembourg. No-one thought that a Luxembourg athlete would win a medal in any event, let alone come first, so no sheet music had been provided for the country's national anthem. Those present at the medals ceremony were eventually treated to an improvised version by the Olympic band.

Mind you, that's nothing compared to the confusion at the 1936 Berlin Games. When Frenchman Louis Hostin won a weightlifting gold, they accidentally raised the Turkish flag – and played the Egyptian national anthem.

★ ★ ★

It was fitting that the new Oriole Park baseball stadium in Baltimore should honour the city's favourite son, the legendary Babe Ruth. A nine-foot-high, 800-pound bronze statue of the great man was commissioned, to take pride of place at the entrance. The sculptor, Susan Leury, began work in 1994. Known for her painstaking attention to detail, Leury was determined to make the likeness as accurate as possible. She talked to numerous experts and fans of Babe Ruth. She studied hundreds of photos of him in action to make sure she captured details such as the exact angle of his hat, the way his belt was fastened and how his laces were tied.

Eventually, after hundreds of hours'

> He's a million-dollar talent with a ten-cent brain.
> – Sportscaster Harry Carayan on baseball star Richie Allen

work the statue was completed. After the ceremonial unveiling, however, it was discovered that Susan had missed one small detail. Her statue of Babe Ruth was right-handed. The man himself was a lefty!

★ ★ ★

James Hunt was once asked to demonstrate the capabilities of a new Mercedes at a press launch at Donington Park. True to form, he put the car through a blistering, high-speed performance on the track that really showed off its handling capabilities. Only when he returned to the pits did Mercedes employees spot smoke billowing from all four wheels. Hunt had forgotten to take the handbrake off during the demonstration…

★ ★ ★

A soldier, who was also a keen gymnast, was guarding four Mirage jet fighters at a Greek air base in February 1981. One of the features of the sleek fighter aircraft is a tapering nose cone that conceals delicate radar equipment and which ends in a long point. The bored sentry was looking to pass the time and since no one was looking, he decided to swing on the point for exercise, practising some of his gymnastic manoeuvres.

He was literally in the swing of things when he heard a loud crack – his weight had bent the nose cone downwards. On investigation the soldier discovered it couldn't be straightened out. There was only one thing to do – he swung on the other three

> He doesn't know the meaning of the word fear. Of course, there are lots of other words he doesn't know either.
> – Sid Gillman, football coach, on one of his players

aircraft, duplicating the damage. He later admitted his crime before a military tribunal, claiming, 'I hoped no-one would notice the difference.'

★ ★ ★

A recent survey carried by *Running* magazine listed the greatest hazards to athletes who train on the road. Surprisingly, these were not things like cars or dogs but rather more static items like brick walls, lamp-posts, scaffolding, trees and even bus shelters.

* * *

Boxer Daniel Caruso had a strange way of preparing himself for a fight; he used to psyche himself up by punching himself in the face. Before the 1992 New York Golden Gloves championship he went too far, breaking his own nose. Doctors examining him ruled that he was unfit to box.

* * *

Racing pigeons can legitimately change hands for thousands of pounds, so the thieves who broke into Bob Hodgson's pigeon loft in Ryton, Tyne and Wear in 1997 and stole 40 birds probably thought they were on to a real winner. However, they hadn't really thought things through.

A few days later, almost all of the birds had flown home again. After all, they were homing pigeons...

'Perhaps this gives you some idea of the level of intelligence of some of the thieves we have to deal with around here,' said an exasperated police spokesman.

* * *

Isadore Irandir played in goal for the Brazilian club Rio Preto but put his faith in God rather than in his teammates – or his own abilities. Before every game he would get down on his knees in the goalmouth and pray for a clean sheet. Sometimes his prayers were heard and sometimes they

> He's accused of being arrogant, unable to cope with the press and a boozer. Sounds like he's got a chance, to me.
> – George Best, talking about Paul Gascoigne in 1988

went unanswered – such as the time when his team played rivals Corinthians. Irandir was still praying when the Brazilian striker Roberto Rivelino took possession and scored with a shot from the half way line.

If that wasn't a spectacle in itself – or the fastest goal ever scored – the keeper's brother exacted revenge for this 'blasphemy' by running on to the pitch and shooting six bullets into the ball.

★ ★ ★

It was the biggest event of the day at the Atlantic City racetrack and all eyes were on Basic Instinct, the hot favourite. He looked proud and confident in the starting gate – every inch a winner. Then the starting gate sprang open and the runners raced forward, jockeying for position – except for Basic Instinct who remained in his gate. His jockey tried everything, urging him on wildly, tugging his main, swatting his flanks with his crop, but nothing could move the race horse. His tail had been shut in the rear stall gate.

★ ★ ★

At match point in the 1964 Wimbledon first-round singles match between Abe Segal and Clark Graebner, Graebner served the ball. To everyone's surprise, the fault wasn't called. Graebner was sure the ball was out. So was everyone else in the crowd. Everyone, that is, except line judge Dorothy Cavis-Brown, who was fast asleep. The photograph of her with legs crossed, arms folded and head lolling to one side was the most

> ❝ If you can't stand the heat in the dressing room, get out of the kitchen. ❞
> – Terry Venables

famous image of that Wimbledon tournament. She claimed it was the sun that sent her to sleep and that she had only had one gin at lunch time. Not surprisingly, she never officiated at Wimbledon again.

* * *

One of the most disappointed athletes of all time must have been the South African runner Johannes Coleman. He was running in the 1938 Natal marathon and desperate to beat the world record of 2 hours 26 minutes 42 seconds. As he stormed down the home stretch in Alexander Park, Pietermaritzburg, his own watch said 2 hours 23 minutes; the record was surely his.

To his horror Coleman discovered that there had been no 'official' time recorded for the run – and therefore his record could not be ratified. It turned out that the timekeeper was not at his post when Coleman crossed the line; he was having a cup of tea in the refreshment tent. All he could do was apologise for his absence, saying that he hadn't expected any of the runners to finish so soon.

* * *

Don't believe everything you hear about German efficiency; the 1974 World Cup Final was delayed because the groundsman had forgotten to put the corner flags in place.

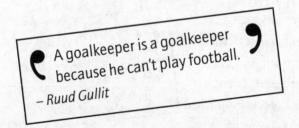

A goalkeeper is a goalkeeper because he can't play football.
– *Ruud Gullit*

CHAPTER 14

Having the Last Word

'The decathlon is nine Mickey Mouse events
and the 1500 metres'
– *Steve Ovett*

World heavyweight boxing champion John L Sullivan wasn't a man who took orders easily, so when a trolley-bus conductor refused to allow Sullivan's beloved dog on board with his master the boxer floored him with one well-aimed punch. Sullivan was taken to court and found guilty of assault. 'Mr Sullivan, I fine you 100 dollars for hitting that man,' said his judge at the trial. 'Do you have anything you want to say?'

Sullivan reached for his wallet and replied, 'Yes, your honour. I'll give you another 200 if you let me hit him again!'

★ ★ ★

Don't argue with the umpire, but if you do, make sure you have the last word. That's sort of what Chicago Cubs outfielder Andre Dawson did when he was fined $1,000 for disputing a call made by umpire Joe West in 1991. He paid by cheque, adding these words to the bottom of it: 'Donation to the blind'.

✴   ✴   ✴

The Italian squad weren't happy with all their facilities at Euro 96 and paid to have them upgraded. The accommodation and training ground were OK; it was just that the mirrors and hairdriers didn't meet their standards.

✴   ✴   ✴

Streakers who disrupt sporting events are usually exhibitionist fans – not the players themselves. An exception to this rule was Dutch player Patrick Deckers, who played for Eindhoven. After being sent off in a match against Helmond Sport, Patrick showed his indignation – and quite a lot more – when he stood on the touchline and waved his private parts at the crowd. He was later sacked by the club who commented that 'showing one's genitalia at a public football match is prohibited by law'.

* * *

Peruvian commentator Mario Sanchez was interviewing the striker Corina after a match, asking if he had considered a way to improve his accuracy after he missed three easy headers in a game. As if to show him, Corina head butted the commentator, knocking him unconscious.

* * *

Muhammad Ali got his real break when world heavyweight champion Sonny 'The Bear' Liston agreed to fight him. Until then he'd ignored Ali, considering him not worth bothering with. Ali launched a determined campaign to antagonise him, even going so far as to put a bear trap in his front garden and driving up and down outside his house, shouting insults out of the car window to wind him up. Riled and incensed, Liston threw down the gauntlet. The bookies gave odds against Clay of 6–1 – and bets were even taken that Liston would kill Ali in the ring. In the event, Liston refused to come out for the seventh.

Liston also lost the rematch when he was knocked out in the first round.

* * *

A different kind of driver was seen in action at the Manor House Hotel golf course at Moretonhampstead, Devon in September 1993. It happened when a window cleaner decided to take revenge against the club,

> People always said I shouldn't be burning my candle at both ends. Maybe that's because they don't have a big enough candle.
> – George Best

161

who, he claimed, owed him money. After long harbouring his grudge, the driver left the road that leads through the course in his Austin Montego, and drove across the thirteenth and fourteenth greens, narrowly avoiding players who promptly scattered in all directions. He then ruined the fourth green by executing a perfect 360-degree handbrake turn on it, and re-joined the public road where he was eventually caught after a chase involving seven police cars and a helicopter.

He was eventually sentenced to eight months in jail and banned from driving for two years. When asked why he had committed the offence he told police, 'I hate fat bastards who play golf,' but added, 'Anyway, it was a good advert for the Montego.'

★ ★ ★

Tennis bad boy Ilie Nastase can swear fluently in six languages. He once threatened umpire Jeremy Shales during a tournament in Bournemouth in 1982, shouting 'Come down off your chair and I will kill you with a ball in the mouth!'

★ ★ ★

Germany's penalty shoot-out win over England at Euro 96 caught the imagination of the Bayer chemical company's local operations in Guatemala. They advertised a new brand of insecticide with the line 'sudden death is a German speciality'. It was swiftly withdrawn after shareholders thought it might be misinterpreted…

> ❝ What's the difference between a puppy and a sportswriter? In six weeks, the puppy stops whining. ❞
> – Mike Ditka, coach of the Chicago Bears

★ ★ ★

German referee Bayram Kaymakci was known for being ruthless about discipline on the football field. Kaymakci would show the yellow or red cards to players for the smallest of infringements or offences. Players hated matches in which he officiated and when striker Osbert Vorwerk got sent off for a foul he protested, refusing to leave the pitch. The referee then pulled out a gun from his shorts and shot Osbert in the head. Thankfully, the bullet just nicked his ear. The ref was then thrown to the ground by Osbert's teammates who refused to carry on until a new official was appointed. Kaymakci was fined and banned for three months but was unrepentant. He told reporters, 'One has to maintain

discipline on the field, otherwise the game doesn't flow properly and children can't enjoy it.'

★   ★   ★

When Margaret Thatcher angrily summoned FA Secretary Ted Croker to 10 Downing Street to demand to know what he planned to do about soccer hooliganism, Croker neatly replied, 'These people are society's problem and we don't want your hooligans at our sport!'

★   ★   ★

An arrogant young bowler once decided to abuse Viv Richards after the great batsman had missed the ball. 'You're meant to hit the ball. You know, that thing that's red and round,' he sneered. Richards answered him by knocking his very next ball out of the ground. 'Since you know what it looks like, you go and get it,' he replied.

★   ★   ★

Do you remember when Emlyn Hughes was cheeky to the Princess Royal on *A Question of Sport?* Well, he was just following in the footsteps of other sportsmen who seemed impervious to royal protocol. When American golfer Walter Hagen played a round with King Edward VIII he was heard to say, 'Eddie – hold the flag, will you?'

American athlete Jim Thorpe won gold medals for the pentathlon and decathlon at the 1912 Olympic Games in

> I know I'm no Kim Basinger – but she can't throw the javelin.
> – Fatima Whitbread

Stockholm. He was presented with the medals by King Gustav of Sweden, who Thorpe greeted with, 'Hi, King!'

Similarly, when Babe Ruth walked across the Washington ball park one summer's day to meet President Harding his opening greeting was, 'Hot as hell, ain't it Prez?'

★   ★   ★

Golfer Max Faulkner was so confident when he played in the 1951 Open that at the start of the final round he signed his autographs, '*Max Faulkner, the 1951 Open Champion*'. Fortunately he did win, by two shots.